# The Investment Onboarding Playbook

*How to Actually Start Investing When Every Guide Assumes You Already Know the Vocabulary*

Daniel Cross

First edition, 2026

Published by Daniel Cross

# Contents

# Foreword

A few years ago, someone I'd known for a while asked me to help her open her first investment account. She was in her thirties, had a stable job, had a few thousand dollars past her emergency fund, and had read four different beginner articles on how to "start investing." Every one told her, in some version of the same sentence, to open a brokerage account and buy a low-cost index fund. Not one told her what a brokerage account actually was, how it differed from her checking account, what "low-cost" meant as a number she could look up, or what button to press once she'd picked one.

We sat down for maybe ninety minutes. Deciding what to invest in took ten minutes, once she understood the vocabulary. The rest went to the vocabulary itself: what a ticker symbol is, what an expense ratio is and why a few tenths of a percent matters over decades, what happens between clicking "buy" and actually owning something, why her account had a cash balance that wasn't invested in anything. None of it was advanced — it was assumed knowledge in every article she'd read, and none of those articles had checked whether the assumption was true.

That gap is the entire reason this book exists. What's missing from most advice isn't the case for investing — it's the layer underneath: the actual mechanics of going from a bank balance to a functioning account, written for someone who has genuinely never done this and doesn't want to be talked down to for not knowing it. This isn't a book about whether to invest — if you've picked it up, you've decided that. It's the manual for the part nobody writes down: what to open, what to fund first, what to buy, and what button to press. Nothing here is a stock tip — a beginner's first need is to stop being confused by the vocabulary long enough to make an ordinary decision and execute it.

That conversation happened more than once, with more than one person, before I sat down to write this — different jobs, different ages, different amounts saved, the same obstacle every time. Nobody had walked them through the mechanics in plain language, start to finish. This book is that same conversation, written down, so it doesn't have to happen one kitchen table at a time.

— Daniel Cross

# Introduction — How to Use This Book

This book teaches one thing: how to go from zero investment accounts to a functioning one, mechanically, from the first login to the first trade to the first year of ordinary maintenance. It isn't a book about which stocks will do well, which sectors are about to move, or how to time a market cycle — nobody can reliably promise any of that, and a book that pretended otherwise wouldn't deserve your trust. It's a book about the specific, learnable, entirely mechanical steps that stand between "I know I should be investing" and an account that's actually open, actually funded, and actually holding something.

This gap is more common, and more embarrassing to admit out loud, than most people assume. Financial media is saturated with advice aimed at people who already have an account — what to buy next, how to rebalance, how to think about a market downturn. Almost none of it is aimed at the person who doesn't have an account at all and doesn't know where to start, because that person is assumed not to exist by the time most financial content gets written. They exist. This book is for them.

Every chapter in this book follows the same shape, matching the rest of this library, on purpose, so you can find what you need fast:

**The situation** — a concrete, realistic scenario. Not a real person, not a case study with a name attached, but a composite built from the kind of onboarding moment that happens constantly, across professions and income levels, in roughly the same shape every time.

**The mechanics** — what's actually happening underneath the decision or the confusion in that scenario. Where the real distinctions sit, what actually varies between two options that look identical, and what genuinely doesn't matter as much as it seems to in the moment.

**The framework** — the actual tool. A checklist, a decision tree, a formula, or a step-by-step sequence you can follow directly, built to be used rather than just read.

**A worked example** — the tool applied start to finish with real, illustrative numbers, so you can see the shape of it in motion rather than just in the abstract.

A rough map of which chapters fit which situation, useful for finding your footing quickly. If you don't have any investment account open yet and the vocabulary itself is the obstacle, start with Chapter 1. If you have some savings set aside and are trying to choose where to actually open an account, Chapter 2 gives you the real criteria. If you're confused about the difference between a 401(k), an IRA, and a plain brokerage account, and what actually happens mechanically inside each one, Chapter 3 is built specifically for that confusion. If you have money to invest and don't know what order to put it into different accounts, Chapter 4 gives you the sequence. If you're wondering whether to buy individual stocks or a fund, and what actually separates the two, Chapter 5 walks through the decision. If someone told you to check a fund's expense ratio and you don't know what that means or why it matters, Chapter 6 makes it concrete. If you have a lump sum and are frozen by the fear of investing it at the wrong moment, Chapter 7 gives you a real schedule for spreading it out. If you've picked an account and a fund but freeze at the actual purchase screen, Chapter 8 walks through the mechanics of placing a trade. If you've been investing for a while and have never checked whether your allocation has drifted, Chapter 9 gives you the triggers for when and how to correct it. And if you want the whole thing distilled into a single month-by-month plan for your first year, Chapter 10 is built to be read in one sitting and then followed for the next twelve months.

You don't need to read this book in order, and you don't need to use every chapter today. Read the chapters that map to where you actually are right now, execute the framework, and come back for the rest as your situation develops. This isn't a book meant to be read once and shelved — it's meant to sit next to your laptop the first time you actually open a brokerage app, and to be reopened a year later when your situation has changed enough that the next chapter finally applies.

A word on what this book won't do. It won't tell you which specific fund, stock, or brokerage to use — the market for all three changes constantly, and a book that named a specific winner would be stale within a few years and, worse, would be giving you a recommendation instead of a method for making your own decision. What it will do is give you the actual criteria for evaluating any brokerage, any fund, and any account type you're looking at right now, so the framework still works long after any specific product mentioned as an example has changed or disappeared entirely.

A word on the scenarios throughout this book: every situation described — the nurse, the physical therapist, the warehouse supervisor, the dental hygienist, and everyone else who appears in these chapters — is a composite, built from the recognizable shape of a common onboarding moment rather than a record of any one real person's exact circumstances. You won't find a name attached to any of them, on purpose. If one of these scenarios lands close to your own situation, that's the point — it's meant to.

A word, too, on how this book treats numbers. Dollar figures, fee percentages, and account limits appear throughout as illustrations of a mechanism, not as claims about current market conditions, current fee schedules, or current contribution limits in any specific year. Brokerage pricing, fund expense ratios, and IRS contribution limits all change — sometimes annually, sometimes more often — and a book that anchored its lessons to a snapshot of 2026 numbers would read as dated within a year or two. What doesn't age is the underlying logic: how an expense ratio compounds, how dollar-cost averaging works structurally, how a funding order of operations is built. Always verify the actual current number — a current expense ratio, a current contribution limit, a current tax rule — directly with your brokerage, plan administrator, or the IRS before acting; the numbers in this book's examples are there to make the mechanics concrete, not to be copied directly into your own plan.

Finally, a note on where this book sits relative to its companion volumes in this library. *The Automatic Wealth System* covers how to build a bank-account structure and automate transfers so saving happens without relying on willpower — it assumes you already know what you're transferring money into. *The Savings Rate Playbook* covers how much to save and, in its chapter on retirement accounts versus accessible savings, how to split that rate between tax-advantaged and taxable vehicles once you already have both kinds of account open. Neither book covers how to actually open an investment account for the first time, choose a brokerage, understand what you're buying, or execute the purchase — that gap is this book's entire territory. If you're arriving here with no investment accounts open at all, start here. If you already have accounts open and funded and are trying to decide how much goes where, those two companion volumes are the better starting point, and you can return here for the specific mechanics of expense ratios, order types, or rebalancing whenever a chapter's topic becomes relevant.

One last practical note before Chapter 1: this book is written for a reader in the United States, since account types, tax treatment, and specific regulatory bodies referenced throughout — the IRS, the SEC, SIPC, FINRA — are U.S.-specific institutions and rules. A reader outside the United States will find the underlying mechanics genuinely transferable — the logic of comparing brokerages, understanding an expense ratio, choosing between a fund and an individual stock, building a funding order of operations, and rebalancing a portfolio all apply regardless of jurisdiction — but the specific account types, contribution limits, and regulatory protections named throughout will differ by country, and should be checked against the equivalent institutions and rules in your own jurisdiction rather than assumed to transfer directly from the U.S.-specific examples used here.

# Chapter 1 — The Zero Point

## What "Opening an Account" Actually Means

### The situation

A nurse in her mid-thirties has eight thousand dollars sitting in a checking account, well past what she needs for her emergency fund, and has known for at least two years that she "should be investing" it. She's read three different beginner guides, all of which tell her, in roughly the same sentence, to open a brokerage account and buy a low-cost index fund. She closes each article with two new problems instead of one: she still doesn't have an account, and she now has a list of terms — ticker symbol, expense ratio, NAV, settlement date — that nobody stopped to define before assuming she already knew them.

This isn't a failure of intelligence or effort. She's competent at her job, manages a household budget without difficulty, and has no trouble reading a dense insurance policy or a medication chart. The problem is specific: financial media, almost universally, is written by and for people who already crossed the exact threshold she's stuck at. The vocabulary that would make the next article legible is treated as background knowledge, not as the actual first lesson — and so the first lesson never gets taught.

## The mechanics

A brokerage account is not a bank account, even though the apps that hold them increasingly look and feel like one. A bank account holds cash, and the bank owes you that cash back on demand — legally, you're a creditor of the bank. A brokerage account holds securities — shares of stock, shares of a fund, bonds — that you actually own, held in what's called "street name" for convenience (meaning the brokerage's name is on the official record, but the shares are legally yours, tracked in your account), plus whatever cash hasn't yet been invested. The brokerage is a custodian, not an owner. If the brokerage itself went out of business, your securities don't disappear — they're protected, up to standard limits, by the Securities Investor Protection Corporation (SIPC), a government-chartered nonprofit that insures brokerage accounts against the failure of the brokerage firm itself, distinct from — and not a substitute for — protection against ordinary investment losses, which SIPC does not cover and no legitimate protection ever does.

A handful of terms account for most of the confusion in every beginner guide that assumes them:

**Ticker symbol** — the short letter code that identifies a specific stock or fund on an exchange, the way a flight number identifies a specific flight. You search this code, not the company or fund's full name, to find and buy something.

**Share** — a single unit of ownership in a stock or fund. You can own one share, a fraction of a share, or thousands, and most modern brokerages now support buying fractional shares — a dollar amount rather than a whole number of shares — which removes what used to be a real barrier to entry for expensive stocks and funds.

**Net asset value (NAV)** — the per-share price of a mutual fund, calculated once per trading day after markets close, based on the total value of everything the fund holds divided by the number of shares outstanding. This is different from how an exchange-traded fund (ETF) or a stock is priced, which happens continuously throughout the trading day as buyers and sellers transact — a distinction that matters more than it sounds and gets its own full treatment in Chapter 8.

**Expense ratio** — the annual fee a fund charges, expressed as a percentage of the money you have invested in it, deducted automatically and continuously rather than billed to you separately. This gets an entire chapter of its own (Chapter 6), because its effect compounds in a way that's easy to underestimate from the small-looking percentage alone.

**Settlement** — the gap between when a trade executes and when it officially, legally finalizes. In the United States, the standard settlement period for most stock and ETF trades is one business day after the trade date, a rule the Securities and Exchange Commission shortened from two business days to one in 2024. Until a trade settles, the shares or cash from it aren't fully available to use for certain purposes, like an immediate withdrawal — a detail that occasionally trips up someone who sells one holding and tries to immediately withdraw the proceeds the same day.

**Cash balance** — the uninvested money sitting in your brokerage account, separate from anything you've actually purchased. This is the detail that catches nearly every first-time investor off guard: depositing money into a brokerage account does not, by itself, invest it in anything. The money sits as cash, earning little or nothing, until you take the additional, separate step of using it to buy something. This single misunderstanding is likely the single most common reason someone "opens an investment account" and, a year later, discovers their money never actually left cash.

## The framework: the five things to know before you open anything

**1. Know what a brokerage account legally is.** A custodial relationship holding securities you own, protected by SIPC against the brokerage's failure, not against market losses. This isn't a bank account with extra steps — it's a fundamentally different kind of account, and knowing that distinction removes a surprising amount of unfounded anxiety about "trusting" a brokerage with your money.

**2. Know that depositing money and investing money are two separate actions.** Funding an account moves cash into it. Buying something is a distinct, additional step you have to take deliberately. No brokerage automatically invests a cash deposit into anything on your behalf unless you've specifically set up a recurring automatic purchase, which Chapter 7 covers directly.

**3. Know the difference between a ticker symbol and a company or fund name.** You'll search and transact using the ticker, not the plain-language name, and mixing up two similarly named tickers is a real, avoidable mistake covered in full in Chapter 8.

**4. Know that a fund's price (NAV or market price) isn't the same as its quality.** A ten-dollar share and a four-hundred-dollar share can represent funds that are functionally identical in what they hold and how they perform per dollar invested — price per share is a function of how the fund happens to be structured, not a signal of value, cost, or performance. This misunderstanding leads some beginners to avoid a genuinely excellent fund because its per-share price looks intimidatingly high, when the actual dollar amount invested is what matters, not the number of shares that amount buys.

**5. Know that "expense ratio" is the single vocabulary term worth understanding before anything else on this list.** Everything else here is about navigating an account. This one directly affects how much of your own money you keep over decades, and it's covered in full in Chapter 6.

## Worked example

The nurse from this chapter's opening sits down with this five-point framework before opening anything. She confirms, first, that a brokerage account is a different legal structure from her checking account, and that the SIPC protection she's read about covers the brokerage's failure, not a market downturn — a distinction that resolves a specific, unspoken worry she'd had about "putting her money somewhere less safe than a bank." She confirms that funding an account and investing the money inside it are two separate steps, which explains why a coworker who "opened an account two years ago" still has an account balance sitting entirely in cash, having never taken the second step. She practices distinguishing a ticker symbol from a fund's plain-language name using her brokerage's search bar before committing any money, so the first time she does it for real isn't also the first time she's ever done it at all. None of this involves buying anything yet — that's Chapter 8's territory. It's simply the vocabulary layer that every guide she'd previously read had silently assumed she'd already cleared.

## Common objections and how to handle them

**"Isn't all of this covered in the brokerage's own onboarding flow when I sign up?"** Partially, and inconsistently. Most brokerages do a reasonable job walking you through the mechanical steps of opening an account — providing your information, linking a bank account, agreeing to disclosures. Very few explain the vocabulary in plain language along the way, because the onboarding flow assumes you're filling out a form, not learning a new domain from scratch. The account-opening flow and the vocabulary education are two separate jobs, and most brokerages only do the first one well.

**"What if I misuse one of these terms in front of someone and look inexperienced?"** Everyone who currently sounds fluent in this vocabulary was, at some point, exactly where you are now. The terms in this chapter aren't a secret handshake — they're a small, learnable glossary, and the gap between not knowing them and knowing them cold is measured in an afternoon, not years.

**"Do I need to understand all of this before I open an account, or can I learn as I go?"** The five points in this chapter's framework are worth understanding before you open anything, because they prevent a specific, common mistake — funding an account and believing you've invested, when you've actually just moved cash from one place to another. Everything past those five points is genuinely fine to learn as you go, and the rest of this book is built to teach it in the order you'll actually need it.

## A short exercise before you open anything

Before opening any account, open a note on your phone or a blank document and write out, in your own words, a one-sentence definition for each of the five terms in this chapter's framework: brokerage account, cash balance versus investing, ticker symbol, share price versus fund quality, and expense ratio. If you can write a clear sentence for all five without looking anything up, you've cleared the vocabulary floor this chapter exists to build, and Chapter 2's brokerage-selection framework is the right next step. If any of the five come up blank, reread that section of this chapter before moving forward — the rest of this book assumes this floor is solid, the same way a hiking guide assumes you already know how to tie your boots.

## A note on the money sitting in your cash balance

One detail worth understanding before you open anything: the uninvested cash sitting in a brokerage account isn't simply inert. Most major brokerages automatically place uninvested cash into what's called a cash sweep — typically a money market fund or a linked bank deposit program — so that cash sitting in the account earns some modest yield rather than sitting completely idle, even before you've made a deliberate investing decision with it. This is a genuine convenience, but it's worth understanding clearly as a distinct thing from actually investing: the yield on a cash sweep is generally far lower than what a diversified stock-and-bond portfolio has historically returned over a long horizon, and it exists to make waiting less costly, not to substitute for the deliberate step of actually buying something. Confirm what your specific brokerage does with uninvested cash — check the account's cash management or sweep settings — so you know exactly what's happening to money that hasn't yet been directed anywhere else.

### Frequently misunderstood point: SIPC protection and market losses are not the same thing

It's worth restating this distinction plainly, since it's the single most common point of confusion in this chapter. SIPC protection exists to make you whole, up to defined limits, if your brokerage itself fails as a business — goes bankrupt, mismanages custody of client securities, or otherwise can't return what it was holding for you. It does not protect you against a fund or stock you own simply declining in value, which is an ordinary, expected feature of investing, not a failure anyone insures against. A beginner who conflates the two sometimes either avoids investing out of a misplaced worry that a market downturn is somehow "unprotected" in a way it shouldn't be, or, less commonly, assumes SIPC coverage means a specific investment can't lose money, which it doesn't claim to guarantee at all. Neither belief is correct, and clearing up the distinction now prevents both mistakes later.

## A note on custodial and joint accounts

Two account variations worth knowing exist, even if neither applies to your immediate situation. A custodial account (in the U.S., typically structured under the Uniform Transfers to Minors Act or the older Uniform Gifts to Minors Act, generally referred to by their initials) lets an adult open and manage an investment account on behalf of a minor, with the assets legally transferring to the minor's own control at the age of majority defined by their state. A joint brokerage account is opened and owned by two people simultaneously — commonly spouses or partners — with both parties typically able to view, fund, and transact on the account, structured under a specific joint-ownership designation your brokerage will ask you to select during opening. Neither of these is more complicated to open than the individual account this chapter has been describing throughout; the difference is entirely in the account's registration and ownership structure, not in any of the vocabulary or mechanics covered elsewhere in this book.

## A note on account security, since it's part of "opening" too

The mechanical act of opening a brokerage account also opens a new surface for account-takeover fraud, and a small handful of security steps are worth treating as part of the opening process itself rather than an afterthought handled later. Enable two-factor authentication the same day you open the account, before funding it — most brokerages support this through a text code, an authenticator app, or a physical security key, and an authenticator app or security key is generally considered more resistant to interception than a text code alone. Use a unique password for the brokerage login, not one reused from another account, since a breach at an unrelated site is a common way brokerage credentials end up compromised through simple password reuse. And treat any unsolicited email or text claiming to be from your brokerage, asking you to click a link and log in, with default suspicion — navigate to the brokerage's app or website directly instead of through a link in a message, a habit that defeats the large majority of phishing attempts aimed at investment accounts. None of this is unique to investing specifically, but a newly funded account is a specific, real target, and the ten minutes it takes to set these protections up at account opening is worth treating as a mandatory step, not an optional one.

## Frequently misunderstood point: a brokerage isn't picking your investments for you by default

A last piece of vocabulary worth clearing up before moving to Chapter 2: opening a brokerage account does not, by itself, mean anyone at the brokerage is actively managing your money or making investment decisions on your behalf, unless you've specifically opted into a managed or advisory service, which typically carries its own separate, clearly disclosed fee. The default, self-directed brokerage account this book describes throughout is exactly that — self-directed, meaning every purchase decision is yours to make, using the frameworks the rest of this book provides. This is worth stating plainly because some beginners assume, incorrectly, that a brokerage account somehow runs itself once opened, which circles directly back to Chapter 1's central warning: opening and funding an account is not the same as investing the money inside it, and no one else is going to take that step for you by default.

## Warning signs you're stuck at the zero point without realizing it

A short, honest list worth checking yourself against before moving on to Chapter 2. You've said "I should really open an account" more than once in the past year without doing it — that's the paralysis this chapter exists to resolve, and it rarely resolves itself without a deliberate push through the vocabulary. You have money sitting in a checking or savings account well beyond what any near-term goal requires, with no specific plan for it — that's opportunity cost accumulating quietly, the exact cost Chapter 6 will later quantify precisely. You've read more than one "beginner" investing article and come away more confused than when you started — that's a sign the article assumed a vocabulary floor you hadn't yet cleared, not a sign you're bad at this. Any of these three, honestly checked, is a specific, resolvable signal that this chapter's five-point framework is worth working through directly, in writing, before moving forward.

## A note on why this vocabulary gap exists in the first place

It's worth understanding, briefly, why this specific gap is so common, since knowing the cause makes it easier to stop blaming yourself for having it. Financial media, overwhelmingly, is written by people for whom this vocabulary became second nature years or decades ago, often through a job, a degree, or simply years of ordinary exposure to the topic. Writing for a reader who has genuinely never encountered any of it requires a specific, deliberate effort to slow down and define terms that feel too basic to the writer to be worth defining — an effort most content, optimized for a broad, already-somewhat-informed audience, simply doesn't make. This isn't a conspiracy or a deliberate gatekeeping effort; it's closer to an accidental blind spot, repeated across nearly every publisher and platform covering this topic, because the people producing the content and the people reviewing it for clarity are, almost by definition, people who cleared this exact hurdle long enough ago to have forgotten what it felt like not to have. Recognizing this pattern is useful beyond investing specifically — it's a good general-purpose explanation for why so much expert-produced content in any technical field quietly assumes a floor of knowledge the actual audience doesn't yet have.

## A second worked example: a reader starting from a genuinely different situation

A different reader — a recently graduated electrical apprentice, in his first year of steady income after several years of part-time and seasonal work — approaches this same chapter from a slightly different starting point than the nurse. He has no confusion about what a bank account is or how a paycheck works, but has genuinely never encountered any of this chapter's five vocabulary terms in any context, financial or otherwise, since nothing in his education or work life has touched on investing directly. He works through the same five-point framework, writing out his own definitions exactly as the chapter's short exercise describes, and finds the third term — the distinction between a ticker symbol and a fund's full name — the one that takes the longest to feel natural, since it initially strikes him as an unnecessary extra layer of abbreviation rather than a useful shorthand. Practicing with his brokerage's search bar, entering a few tickers for well-known, familiar companies before ever making a purchase, resolves this specific confusion within a single sitting. His path through this chapter looks slightly different from the nurse's — different term proved hardest, different amount of prior exposure — but the destination, a working, applied fluency in these five terms, is identical, which is the point of building the framework around the vocabulary itself rather than around any single reader's specific background.

## Common objections and how to handle them

- **"What if I still feel confused after working through the five-point framework once?"** One pass through unfamiliar vocabulary rarely produces total, permanent fluency, and that's a normal, expected part of learning any new domain rather than a sign this chapter's approach isn't working for you specifically. Revisit the specific term still causing friction, apply it directly inside a real brokerage's search and account interface even before funding anything, and give it a second pass a day or two later — vocabulary that's been used once in a concrete context tends to stick considerably better on a second exposure than it did on the first, purely explanatory pass.

**"Is it normal to still feel nervous about opening an account even after understanding all five terms?"** Yes, and it's worth distinguishing this nervousness clearly from the confusion this chapter is built to resolve. Confusion is about not understanding what something means; nervousness about a first financial decision, even a well-understood one, is a separate, entirely ordinary feeling that doesn't require a vocabulary fix to address — the account-opening process itself, and the small, reversible nature of most of the decisions involved (a brokerage can be changed later, a fund can be swapped later), tends to resolve on its own once the first account is actually open and the abstract fear meets the comparatively mundane reality of an ordinary online form.

# Chapter 2 — Choosing a Brokerage

## The criteria that actually matter

### The situation

A physical therapist has cleared the vocabulary hurdle from Chapter 1 and is ready to open an account, but freezes at a different obstacle: there are several major brokerages, each with an app, each claiming to be the simplest or the best for beginners, and no obvious way to tell them apart. She spends an evening reading comparison articles that mostly rehash the same six brokerage names in different orders, none of which explain what she should actually be checking for in her specific situation. She closes her laptop having made no decision, which functionally means the decision defaults to "not yet" — the most expensive option of all, since every month unopened is a month of missed growth.

### The mechanics

For most of the history of retail brokerages, trading commissions were a real differentiator — some firms charged per trade, some charged less, and the difference genuinely mattered to an active investor. That's no longer the primary axis of comparison. Commission-free trading on stocks and ETFs became the industry standard among major retail brokerages over the past several years, which means the thing beginners most often ask about first — "which one is cheapest to trade with" — is now close to a non-issue across the major players. The real differences that matter for a first-time investor sit elsewhere, in places a commission comparison never looks.

The first real differentiator is account type availability. Not every brokerage offers every account type — some specialize in retirement accounts, some in general taxable brokerage accounts, and confirming that a given brokerage actually offers the specific account type you need (covered fully in Chapter 3) before you commit to it saves a genuinely annoying account-transfer process later.

The second is fund availability and cost, specifically whether the brokerage offers its own low-cost, broadly diversified index funds or ETFs, and what those funds' expense ratios actually are. Many large brokerages have built genuinely excellent, extremely low-cost in-house index fund and ETF lineups, and using a brokerage's own fund family sometimes comes with small additional conveniences — no transaction fee when buying the brokerage's own funds, for instance — that funds from an outside provider might not carry at that same brokerage.

The third is the minimum investment required, which differs meaningfully between mutual funds and ETFs. Many mutual funds carry a minimum initial investment — commonly a few hundred to a few thousand dollars, though this varies fund to fund and firm to firm — below which you simply cannot buy in at all. ETFs, by contrast, trade like a stock: you can typically buy as little as one share, and with fractional-share support now widely available, often far less than one full share in dollar terms. For a beginner starting with a modest amount, this distinction alone can determine which vehicle is actually accessible on day one.

The fourth is the practical experience of using the platform itself — not a cosmetic preference, but a genuine factor in whether you'll actually use the account consistently. A confusing, cluttered interface is a real form of friction that can quietly discourage the very habit this whole book is trying to help you build.

The fifth, easy to overlook until it matters, is how easy or costly it is to leave. Transferring an account from one brokerage to another — an "ACATS transfer," named for the Automated Customer Account Transfer Service that handles it — is generally possible, but some brokerages charge an outgoing transfer fee, sometimes a meaningful flat amount, specifically to discourage you from leaving. This isn't a reason to avoid a brokerage that charges one, since a one-time fee years down the road is a minor cost against a well-chosen platform, but it's worth knowing about in advance rather than discovering it unpleasantly the day you decide to switch.

## The framework: the six-point brokerage scorecard

Before opening an account, check each candidate brokerage against these six criteria, not in the order they're marketed to you, but in the order they actually matter to a first-time investor:

**1. Does it offer the account type I actually need?** (Chapter 3 will help you determine this.) A brokerage that doesn't offer the specific account type you need is disqualified regardless of how well it scores on everything else.

**2. What's the expense ratio on its core low-cost index fund or ETF options?** Look specifically at a broad market index fund or ETF — the kind of holding Chapter 5 will walk you toward as a sensible core position — and compare its expense ratio across your candidate brokerages. Differences here, though they look tiny on the page, compound meaningfully over decades, as Chapter 6 demonstrates directly.

**3. What's the minimum initial investment for the specific fund I'm likely to start with?** If you're starting with a modest amount, confirm whether your intended first purchase is even accessible — an ETF's fractional-share support often clears this bar more easily than a mutual fund's flat dollar minimum.

**4. Does it support automatic recurring purchases?** This single feature is what makes the dollar-cost-averaging schedule in Chapter 7 something you can set up once and let run, rather than something you have to remember to do manually every month. Confirm it exists and how it's configured before you need it.

**5. Is the platform something you can actually navigate without dread?** Spend ten minutes in a demo mode or a free trial account, if available, before committing. This is a real criterion, not a soft one — a platform you avoid opening is a platform that quietly undermines every other good decision in this book.

**6. What does it cost, structurally, to leave later?** Check for an outgoing transfer fee, not as a dealbreaker, but as informed context. A well-chosen brokerage rarely needs to be left, but knowing the exit cost in advance is simply due diligence, the same way you'd check a lease's early-termination clause before signing it, not because you plan to break it, but because informed decisions account for the whole picture.

## Worked example

The physical therapist applies the six-point scorecard to two brokerages she's narrowed her search to. Both offer the account type she needs (a standard taxable brokerage account, plus a Roth IRA she plans to open once she's clarified account types in Chapter 3) and both offer broad market index ETFs with expense ratios well under a tenth of a percent — a near-wash on cost. The real difference she finds is in the fourth and fifth criteria: one brokerage's recurring-purchase feature only supports whole-share purchases, meaning she can't automate a fixed dollar amount into an ETF trading well above her monthly contribution size without leaving cash unused each cycle, while the other supports fractional-share recurring purchases in a fixed dollar amount, which fits her $300-a-month plan exactly. She also spends fifteen minutes in each app and finds one meaningfully easier to navigate, with clearer labeling around cash balance versus invested balance — directly resolving the exact confusion Chapter 1 flagged as the most common beginner mistake. She opens the account with the second brokerage, not because the first was a bad choice in absolute terms, but because it scored lower on the two criteria that mattered most for her specific situation.

## Common objections and how to handle them

**"Does it matter which brokerage I pick if they're all pretty similar now?"** Among major, well-established, SIPC-member brokerages, the floor has genuinely risen —

you're unlikely to make a catastrophic choice among the large, reputable options. But "unlikely to be catastrophic" isn't the same as "doesn't matter," and the six-point scorecard exists specifically to find the differences that do matter for your specific situation, even among broadly similar candidates.

**"Should I pick a brokerage my friend or family member already uses?"** Familiarity has real value — someone who can walk you through their own app in person is a genuine convenience, and it's a legitimate factor to weight. But it shouldn't override the six-point scorecard entirely; run their recommendation through the same criteria rather than adopting it uncritically, since their situation and account needs may not match yours exactly.

**"What if I pick wrong and want to switch brokerages later?"** This is genuinely fixable, via the ACATS transfer process mentioned above, which moves your existing holdings to a new brokerage without requiring you to sell and repurchase (avoiding an unnecessary taxable event in a taxable account, and avoiding being out of the market during the transfer). It's a mild hassle, not a disaster, and it's real information worth having in advance rather than a reason to over-deliberate the initial choice past the point of usefulness.

## A note on robo-advisors as a distinct category

A separate category deserves its own mention here: automated investment platforms, often called robo-advisors, which build and manage a diversified portfolio on your behalf based on a short questionnaire about your goals and risk tolerance, typically for a small additional annual fee layered on top of the underlying funds' own expense ratios. These can be a reasonable option for someone who has cleared this chapter's vocabulary and selection hurdles but genuinely doesn't want to make ongoing fund-selection and rebalancing decisions themselves — the tradeoff is a modest additional fee in exchange for automated decision-making. This book's remaining chapters, particularly Chapter 5's fund-selection framework and Chapter 9's rebalancing triggers, are written for the self-directed path, since that path is where the mechanical vocabulary gap this book addresses is most acute. If a robo-advisor genuinely fits your situation better than the self-directed approach, the account-type mechanics in Chapter 3 and the funding order of operations in Chapter 4 still apply identically — only the fund-selection and rebalancing chapters become less directly relevant, since the platform handles that layer for you.

## A short exercise before opening an account

Pick two or three candidate brokerages and build a simple table with the six scorecard criteria as rows and each brokerage as a column. Fill in what you can find from each brokerage's own website within twenty minutes — most of this information is published openly, since brokerages compete on exactly these points even when their marketing emphasizes other things. Leave any cell blank if you genuinely can't find the answer after a reasonable search, and treat a brokerage that makes basic fee and account information hard to find as a mild negative signal on the fifth criterion, platform usability, since transparency about cost is itself a form of good platform design.

## Frequently misunderstood point: "commission-free" isn't the same as "free"

Commission-free trading removed one real cost, but it didn't remove every cost, and treating a brokerage's marketing around

"$0 commissions" as proof that a given trade costs you nothing at all is a mistake worth correcting directly. A bid-ask spread — the small, ordinary gap between what buyers are willing to pay and what sellers are willing to accept for a security at any given moment — still exists on every trade, commission or no commission, and functions as a real, if usually small, embedded cost. Some brokerages also generate revenue through a practice called payment for order flow, where routing your trade to a specific market maker generates a small payment to the brokerage, a legal and disclosed practice that doesn't cost you a visible fee but is worth knowing exists as part of how a "free" trade is actually being monetized on the brokerage's side. None of this should discourage you from using a commission-free brokerage — for a widely traded index fund or ETF, per Chapter 8's discussion of liquidity, these embedded costs are typically negligible. It's simply worth understanding that "commission-free" describes one specific cost being removed, not every cost.

## A second worked example: three brokerages, three different weak points

A separate first-time investor runs three candidate brokerages through the six-point scorecard and finds each one strong on different criteria and weak on a different one. The first offers an excellent, low-cost proprietary index fund lineup and a genuinely easy-to-navigate app, but doesn't support fractional-share recurring purchases, which matters for his specific $150-a-month contribution plan into a fund trading well above that price per share. The second supports fractional-share automation cleanly and offers a wide selection of low-cost funds from multiple providers, but its mobile app is cluttered enough that he struggles to find his own cash balance without several taps, a real usability cost per the fifth criterion. The third scores well across all six criteria but charges a meaningful outgoing transfer fee, a minor consideration given he has no near-term plan to switch but worth factoring in as a tiebreaker against the second option, which charges none. He selects the second brokerage, weighting the fractional-share automation as decisive for his specific contribution size, while making a mental note to spend a few extra minutes learning the app's less intuitive navigation rather than treating that friction as disqualifying on its own.

## A note on account minimums to open, separate from fund minimums

Distinct from the per-fund minimum investment discussed earlier in this chapter, some brokerages historically required a minimum deposit simply to open an account at all, regardless of what you intended to buy with it. This practice has become far less common among major retail brokerages, many of which now allow an account to be opened with no minimum deposit whatsoever, but it's still worth confirming directly for any brokerage you're seriously considering, particularly a smaller or more specialized firm outside the largest, most widely used platforms — a $0-minimum claim in marketing material is generally accurate for the major players, but verifying it directly for your specific candidate avoids an unwelcome surprise partway through the account-opening flow.

## A note on funding an account, mechanically

Once a brokerage account is open, moving money into it typically happens one of a few ways, worth understanding before you're staring at the funding screen for the first time. An electronic bank transfer (commonly called an ACH transfer in the U.S.) links your checking account and moves money in a few business days, and is the most common, lowest-cost method for an ordinary deposit. A wire transfer moves money same-day but often carries a fee, charged by the sending bank, the receiving brokerage, or both — generally worth using only when speed genuinely matters, not as a routine funding method. A check, mailed or deposited via a mobile scan, remains an option at most brokerages but is slower than an ACH transfer and largely unnecessary given how widely electronic transfers are now supported. For the recurring, automated contributions this book builds toward throughout — particularly the dollar-cost-averaging schedule in Chapter 7 — an ACH-linked recurring transfer, set up once, is the mechanism nearly every reader of this book will actually use on an ongoing basis.

## A note on how long a brand-new account actually takes to become usable

A specific, practical detail worth setting expectations around: opening a brokerage account is rarely instantaneous from application to fully funded and ready to trade. The application and identity-verification step is often quick, sometimes completing within minutes, but the first bank-linked funding transfer, per the note above, can take a few business days to clear before the cash is available to invest. A first-time investor who expects to open an account and place a trade within the same hour sometimes experiences this short waiting period as a sign something has gone wrong, when it's simply the ordinary mechanical timeline of a first deposit clearing through the banking system. Planning for this delay in advance — expecting a few business days between funding and your first trade — avoids the unnecessary alarm of watching a "pending" balance sit unavailable for a short stretch that's entirely normal.

## A note on identity verification during account opening

Every legitimate U.S. brokerage is required, under federal customer-identification rules tied to broader anti-money-laundering regulation, to verify your identity before opening an account — typically requesting your legal name, address, date of birth, and Social Security number or equivalent taxpayer identification number, and sometimes a photo of a government-issued ID for additional verification. This isn't unique to any one brokerage or a sign of unusual scrutiny; it's a standard, universal requirement across the entire industry, and a brokerage that skipped this step entirely would itself be a red flag worth avoiding. Expect to provide this information during account opening, and expect it to be handled through the brokerage's own secure, encrypted process rather than an email or a phone call — a legitimate brokerage will never ask you to send this information through an unsecured channel, a detail worth keeping in mind alongside the phishing guidance covered elsewhere in this chapter.

## A note on confirming a brokerage is a genuine, regulated firm

Before opening an account anywhere, confirm your candidate brokerage is a registered broker-dealer, a status that, in the United States, is verifiable directly through the Financial Industry Regulatory Authority's (FINRA) free, publicly available BrokerCheck tool, which lists a firm's registration status, history, and any disciplinary actions on record. This is a genuinely quick check, taking a few minutes, and it's worth doing specifically for any brokerage that isn't already a widely recognized, major name, since it's the single most reliable way to confirm a firm is legitimately regulated rather than an unregistered or fraudulent operation designed to look like one. Pairing this check with confirming the firm's SIPC membership, discussed in Chapter 1, gives you two independent, verifiable data points confirming a brokerage's legitimacy before a single dollar of your money goes anywhere near it.

## Common objections and how to handle them

**"What if the brokerage with the best scorecard results is one I've never heard of?"** Brand recognition and quality aren't the same thing, and a lesser-known brokerage can genuinely outscore a household name on this chapter's specific criteria. That said, unfamiliarity is a legitimate reason for extra diligence, not automatic disqualification — run the FINRA BrokerCheck verification above, confirm SIPC membership directly, and read a handful of recent, specific user reviews focused on the practical mechanics this chapter cares about (fund availability, app usability, transfer costs) rather than generic star ratings, before committing meaningful money to an unfamiliar platform.

**"Does it matter if a brokerage is a subsidiary of a larger financial company?"** Not materially for the purposes of this chapter's scorecard — many major, well-regarded brokerages operate as part of a larger parent financial company, and the six-point criteria in this chapter apply identically regardless of a firm's corporate structure. What matters is the specific account-level features, fund lineup, and fee structure the brokerage itself offers, not how its ownership is organized above that layer.

## A note on the difference between a brokerage and a bank offering brokerage services

Some traditional banks now offer a brokerage account alongside their usual checking and savings products, generally through a separately registered brokerage arm operating under the bank's brand. This can be a genuine convenience — viewing a checking account and a brokerage account in one login, moving money between them instantly rather than waiting on an external bank transfer — and it's worth weighing as a real factor in the fifth scorecard criterion, platform usability, if you already bank somewhere that offers this. It's worth confirming, though, that the bank's brokerage arm still clears this chapter's other five criteria on its own merits rather than being selected purely for the convenience of a shared login — a bank's brokerage division doesn't automatically match a dedicated brokerage's fund selection, expense ratios, or automation features simply because it shares a parent company, and each of those should still be checked directly rather than assumed.

# Chapter 3 — Account Types, Mechanically

## Taxable, IRA, and employer plans — what actually differs underneath the names

### The situation

A warehouse supervisor has heard the terms "401(k)," "Roth IRA," "traditional IRA," and "brokerage account" used interchangeably in casual conversation for years, as though they're roughly the same thing with different names attached. He has a vague sense that a 401(k) is "for retirement" and a "brokerage account" is "for regular investing," but couldn't explain the actual mechanical difference between a Roth and a traditional IRA if asked directly, and has never opened either because he doesn't know which one he's supposed to want.

### The mechanics

Every account type in this chapter exists to answer one underlying question differently: when does the government tax this money, and under what conditions can you take it back out? Everything else — contribution limits, eligibility rules, employer involvement — follows from that one structural choice.

**A taxable brokerage account** is the simplest structure and the one Chapters 1 and 2 have been describing by default. You fund it with money you've already paid income tax on. There's no special tax advantage on the way in, no restriction on when you can withdraw, and no penalty for taking money out at any time, for any reason. What you do owe tax on is any investment gain — generally at capital gains tax rates when you sell a holding for more than you paid for it, and on dividends as they're paid, both governed by current IRS rules that are worth confirming directly rather than assumed. The appeal of this account type is total flexibility: no age restriction, no early-withdrawal penalty, no limit on how much you can contribute in a given year. The tradeoff is that you get none of the tax benefits the next two account types offer.

**A traditional IRA (Individual Retirement Account)** and an employer-sponsored **traditional 401(k)** share the same core tax mechanic, differing mainly in how you access them. Contributions to a traditional account are typically made with pre-tax dollars — for a 401(k), this usually happens automatically through payroll deduction before income tax is calculated on that portion of your paycheck; for a traditional IRA opened independently at a brokerage, the contribution may be tax-deductible depending on your income and whether you or a spouse has access to an employer plan, a rule worth confirming against current IRS guidance for your specific situation. The money then grows tax-deferred — no tax owed on gains or dividends while it stays inside the account — and you pay ordinary income tax on withdrawals once you actually take the money out, typically in retirement. Withdraw before the standard retirement age (59½, under current rules) and you generally owe both the ordinary income tax and an additional early-withdrawal penalty, with a defined, narrow set of exceptions.

**A Roth IRA** and an employer-sponsored **Roth 401(k)** invert that mechanic. Contributions are made with money you've already paid income tax on — no upfront deduction — but growth and qualified withdrawals in retirement are entirely tax-free, with no tax owed on decades of accumulated gains, a genuinely significant benefit for money that has a long time to compound. Roth IRAs, specifically, come with a valuable, often under-known feature: your original contributions (though generally not the earnings on top of them) can typically be withdrawn at any time, for any reason, without tax or penalty, since you already paid tax on that money before it went in. This makes a Roth IRA structurally more flexible than a traditional account for someone who might conceivably need access to their contributed principal before retirement age, even though it's still intended and best used as a long-horizon retirement vehicle.

The mechanical difference between an IRA and a 401(k), independent of the traditional-versus-Roth question, is about who administers the account and how you access it. A 401(k) is sponsored by an employer, funded automatically through payroll, often paired with an employer matching contribution (a genuinely significant, effectively guaranteed additional return, covered directly in Chapter 4), and typically limited to a specific menu of investment options the employer's plan has selected — you generally can't buy just any fund inside a 401(k) the way you could inside a self-directed IRA. An IRA is opened independently, at any brokerage of your choosing, funded by you directly rather than through payroll, and gives you full access to that brokerage's entire fund and stock lineup rather than a limited employer-selected menu. Both traditional and Roth versions of both account types carry annual contribution limits set and periodically adjusted by the IRS — always confirm the current figure directly with the IRS or your plan administrator rather than assuming a number that may be out of date by the time you're reading this.

## The framework: opening each account type, mechanically

**Opening a 401(k)** isn't something you do at a brokerage directly — it happens through your employer's HR or payroll system, typically during onboarding or an open-enrollment period, where you select a contribution percentage (often with an option to choose traditional, Roth, or a split between both, depending on the specific plan) and select investments from the plan's provided menu. If you're employed and haven't done this yet, the first mechanical step is confirming with HR or your payroll platform that this hasn't already been set up by default and that you know your current contribution percentage.

**Opening an IRA (traditional or Roth)** is done directly at a brokerage of your choosing, using the exact process from Chapter 2 — select the brokerage, then within that brokerage's account-opening flow, select "IRA" as the account type and choose traditional or Roth. You'll need to confirm eligibility, since Roth IRA contributions phase out above certain income levels under current IRS rules, worth checking directly against your own income before assuming eligibility. Funding happens by transferring money directly from a linked bank account, the same mechanical process as funding a taxable brokerage account, just routed into this differently-taxed account type instead.

**Opening a taxable brokerage account** is the simplest of the three mechanically — no eligibility rules, no employer involvement, no contribution limit — and follows the exact process from Chapters 1 and 2 directly.

A decision worth making explicitly, and distinct from the funding-priority question Chapter 4 answers: which account type should you open first, mechanically, given your specific employment situation? If your employer offers a 401(k) with any matching contribution at all, confirming that account is set up and at minimum capturing the full match is the first mechanical action, regardless of what else you eventually open, for reasons Chapter 4 covers in depth. If you don't have access to an employer plan, or want a self-directed account with full control over fund selection, an IRA — Roth if you're eligible and expect your tax rate in retirement to be similar to or higher than it is now, traditional if you expect it to be meaningfully lower — is typically the next account to open. A taxable brokerage account becomes relevant once you're contributing beyond what tax-advantaged space allows, or want money accessible before retirement age for a goal with a nearer-term timeline, a distinction covered in full in this library's companion volume on savings rate, specifically its chapter on retirement accounts versus accessible savings.

## Worked example

The warehouse supervisor from this chapter's opening confirms with HR that his employer offers a 401(k) with a partial match, which he had never actually enrolled in, having assumed — incorrectly — that it required a minimum tenure he hadn't yet reached. He enrolls, selects a Roth 401(k) contribution option since it's offered and he expects to be in a similar or higher tax bracket by retirement given his current early-career trajectory, and sets an initial contribution percentage sufficient to capture the full employer match. Separately, at a brokerage he selected using Chapter 2's scorecard, he opens a Roth IRA — confirming first that his income falls under the current eligibility threshold — to hold additional retirement savings beyond what the 401(k)'s limited fund menu offers, giving him access to a broader, self-selected set of low-cost index funds. He does not yet open a taxable brokerage account, since he has no savings currently earmarked for a goal nearer-term than retirement and hasn't yet maxed out his available tax-advantaged space — a funding-order decision that Chapter 4 covers directly.

## Common objections and how to handle them

**"How do I know whether I'll be in a higher or lower tax bracket in retirement, to choose between Roth and**

**traditional?"** Nobody knows this with certainty, since it depends on future tax law and your future income, both genuinely unpredictable decades out. A reasonable default for someone early in their career, with income likely to grow, is to lean Roth, since paying tax now at a presumably lower current rate and locking in tax-free growth on decades of future gains is often favorable. Someone later in their career, at peak earning years and a correspondingly higher current tax rate, often leans traditional, deferring tax to retirement when income, and therefore the tax rate applied, may be lower. This is a genuinely individual judgment call, and where the stakes are large, worth a conversation with a tax professional rather than a rule of thumb alone.

**"Can I have more than one of these account types at once?"** Yes, and it's common — a 401(k) through an employer, a separate IRA at a brokerage of your choosing, and a taxable brokerage account can all exist simultaneously, each serving a different structural job. This chapter's framework is about understanding what each one mechanically does, not about picking a single one to the exclusion of the others.

**"What if my employer doesn't offer a 401(k) at all?"** Then the 401(k) step in this chapter's framework simply doesn't apply to you, and an IRA — opened directly at a brokerage using Chapter 2's process — becomes your first tax-advantaged account. This is a common and entirely workable situation, particularly for freelancers, contractors, and employees of smaller companies without a retirement benefit; it just means your entire tax-advantaged contribution has to be self-directed rather than partly automated through payroll.

## A note on what this chapter deliberately doesn't cover

This chapter answers a mechanical question — what each account type is, how it's taxed, and how to actually open it — deliberately, and stops short of answering how much of your available savings should go into each one, or how to weigh a near-term accessible-savings goal against a long-horizon tax-advantaged one. That allocation question is covered in full, with a dedicated goal-timeline framework, in this library's companion volume on savings rate. The two questions are related but distinct: this chapter tells you what exists and how to open it; the companion volume tells you how much of your money should go where, once it exists.

## A short exercise before opening an account

Write down every account type you currently have access to: an employer plan, if offered, and whether you're currently enrolled and at what contribution percentage; eligibility for a Roth IRA based on your current income; and whether you have any existing taxable brokerage holdings already. For anything you have access to but haven't opened, note the specific mechanical reason — genuinely never gotten around to it, uncertain about Roth-versus-traditional, unsure about eligibility. Nearly every real barrier at this stage turns out to be a specific, answerable question rather than a genuine obstacle, and naming it precisely is usually the fastest way to resolve it.

## A note on account types for the self-employed

Everything in this chapter's framework assumes either a traditional employer relationship or a fully independent IRA, but a meaningful number of readers work for themselves, and self-employment opens access to a different set of tax-advantaged account types worth knowing about specifically.

A Simplified Employee Pension (SEP) IRA allows a self-employed person or small-business owner to contribute a percentage of net self-employment income, generally with a substantially higher contribution ceiling than a standard IRA, administered through a brokerage in much the same mechanical way as opening a regular IRA. A Solo 401(k), available to a business owner with no employees other than a spouse, functions similarly to an employer-sponsored 401(k) but is self-administered, and can, depending on income, allow for a combination of employee and employer-style contributions that in some cases exceeds what a SEP IRA alone permits. Both account types carry their own specific eligibility rules and contribution formulas, set and periodically adjusted by the IRS, and are genuinely worth a conversation with a tax professional to confirm which structure fits a specific self-employment situation best — the mechanical point for this chapter is simply that self-employment doesn't mean tax-advantaged investing is off the table; it means a different, generally more flexible set of account types becomes available in place of an employer 401(k).

## A note on what happens to a 401(k) when you leave a job

A common, avoidable point of confusion: a 401(k) doesn't disappear, freeze permanently, or get automatically cashed out simply because you leave the employer that sponsored it, though what happens next depends on the choice you make. Generally, you have several mechanical options — leave the account where it is, if your former employer's plan allows it and the balance is above a certain minimum; roll it directly into a new employer's 401(k), if the new plan accepts incoming rollovers; or roll it into an IRA at a brokerage of your choosing, giving you the same broad, self-directed fund selection an IRA offers under Chapter 3's framework, in place of a former employer's limited plan menu. The mechanically important detail is the difference between a direct rollover, where the money moves institution to institution without ever passing through your own hands, and an indirect rollover, where a check is issued to you personally and you have a strict, narrow window — 60 days, under current IRS rules — to deposit the full amount into a new qualifying account or risk the entire balance being treated as a taxable withdrawal, plus a potential early-withdrawal penalty if you're under the standard retirement age. A direct rollover avoids this risk entirely and is, for nearly everyone, the simpler and safer mechanical choice when moving retirement funds between institutions.

## Frequently misunderstood point: "tax-advantaged" doesn't mean "invested for you"

A specific confusion worth clearing up before Chapter 4 builds on this chapter's account types: opening a Roth IRA, a traditional IRA, or enrolling in a 401(k) establishes the tax treatment of the account, but it does not, on its own, determine what the money inside that account is actually invested in. An IRA opened at a brokerage generally starts as an empty shell holding uninvested cash, exactly like the taxable account described in Chapter 1, requiring the same separate, deliberate purchase decision covered fully in Chapters 5 through 8. A 401(k) is a partial exception worth flagging specifically: many employer plans now default new enrollees into a pre-selected investment, commonly a target-date fund matched to an assumed retirement year, meaning a 401(k) contribution is often actually invested in something from the first payroll deduction, unlike a self-directed IRA or taxable account. Confirming whether your specific 401(k) has an active default investment, and what that default actually is, is worth doing directly through your plan's own documentation rather than assuming either outcome.

## A note on required minimum distributions

A mechanical detail relevant primarily to traditional (not Roth) tax-advantaged accounts, worth knowing about even decades before it applies: once you reach a specific age defined by current IRS rules, traditional IRA and traditional 401(k) accounts generally require you to begin withdrawing a minimum amount each year, calculated by a formula based on account balance and life expectancy, whether or not you actually need the money at that time. This rule exists because the government deferred tax on this money at contribution and needs it to eventually be taxed as ordinary income upon withdrawal, and it doesn't apply, under current rules, to Roth IRAs during the original account owner's lifetime — one further mechanical distinction beyond the contribution-side tax treatment already covered in this chapter's core mechanics section, worth being aware of as one more input into the traditional-versus-Roth decision, though the specific age and formula should always be confirmed directly against current IRS guidance given how often such rules are adjusted.

## A short exercise before opening a second or third account type

If you already have one account type open from a prior job or an earlier attempt at investing, list every account you currently hold, in writing, next to which of this chapter's three structural categories it belongs to — taxable, traditional tax-advantaged, or Roth tax-advantaged. For each one, confirm you actually know which category it falls into, since it's genuinely common for someone to hold an account for years without being fully certain whether it's a traditional or Roth structure. If any account's category is unclear, your brokerage's account summary page or a recent statement will state it explicitly, usually right in the account's official name or registration details, and confirming it now prevents a compounding error later, particularly when Chapter 4's funding order of operations depends on knowing exactly what kind of tax-advantaged space you already have available.

## A note on why the tax mechanics in this chapter matter more than they first appear to

It's worth pausing on why this chapter treated the traditional-versus-Roth distinction as genuinely mechanical rather than a minor detail, since the size of the effect is easy to underestimate from the description alone. Over a multi-decade investing horizon, the difference between paying tax on contributions now versus paying tax on a much larger, compounded balance decades later is a real, structurally significant difference in outcome, not a rounding error — which is exactly why this chapter treated it as core mechanics rather than an optional refinement. The specific, correct choice between the two depends on a genuinely individual forecast of your own future tax rate, which nobody can know with certainty, but understanding that the choice itself carries real weight is worth internalizing clearly before treating it as an afterthought during account opening.

## A worked example: comparing a Roth and a traditional contribution mechanically, side by side

To make the mechanical difference concrete: someone contributing $6,000 to a traditional IRA in a year they're taxed at a 22% marginal rate effectively reduces their current taxable income by that $6,000, producing an immediate tax reduction of roughly $1,320 in that specific year (a simplified illustration, not accounting for the full complexity of marginal tax brackets). That same $6,000 then grows tax-deferred, and every dollar withdrawn in retirement is taxed as ordinary income at whatever rate applies then. Contributing the same $6,000 to a Roth IRA instead produces no current-year tax reduction — the $1,320 stays with the IRS this year — but the entire balance, including every dollar of growth accumulated over the following decades, comes out completely tax-free in retirement, provided the withdrawal meets the account's qualifying conditions. Neither version is universally better; the traditional version effectively borrows a lower tax rate today for an unknown tax rate later, while the Roth version locks in today's rate permanently in exchange for giving up this year's tax reduction. Running this exact comparison against your own current marginal tax rate and your own best guess at a future one is the concrete version of the judgment call this chapter has described throughout.

## A note on income limits and the mechanics of eligibility

This chapter has mentioned Roth IRA income eligibility limits at several points without dwelling on the mechanics, and it's worth closing with a direct, practical description of how that eligibility actually works, since it's a common point of confusion for a reader whose income has grown enough to make it newly relevant. Roth IRA eligibility phases out over a specific income range defined by current IRS rules, based on modified adjusted gross income and tax filing status — below the phase-out range, the full contribution is allowed; within it, an allowed contribution amount is reduced on a sliding scale; above it, direct Roth IRA contributions aren't permitted at all for that tax year. For a reader whose income sits above this threshold, a traditional IRA remains available regardless of income (though the tax deductibility of the contribution may itself be limited if you or a spouse has access to an employer plan, a separate rule worth checking directly), and a specific, more advanced mechanism — sometimes informally called a "backdoor" contribution, involving a nondeductible traditional IRA contribution followed by a conversion to Roth — exists for higher-income earners who want Roth-style tax treatment despite exceeding the direct contribution limit. This mechanism carries specific tax-reporting requirements and potential complications depending on whether you hold other traditional IRA balances, and is genuinely worth executing with a tax professional's direct guidance rather than attempting from a general description alone, given how easy it is to trigger an unintended tax consequence if existing traditional IRA balances aren't accounted for correctly in the conversion.

# Chapter 4 — The Order of Operations

## What to fund first

### The situation

A dental hygienist has just cleared Chapter 3's account-type confusion and has, in principle, access to an employer 401(k) with a partial match, eligibility for a Roth IRA, and the ability to open a taxable brokerage account. She has $400 a month she's ready to commit to investing and no idea what order to put it into these three now-understood account types. Every guide she's read gives a different answer, several of them contradicting each other outright, and she's genuinely worried about getting the sequence wrong in some way that costs her real money.

### The mechanics

The good news, largely absent from the conflicting guides she's read, is that this sequence is one of the more settled, non-controversial pieces of practitioner guidance in personal finance — the disagreement in what she's read is more about presentation than about the underlying logic, which holds up consistently once you understand why each step sits where it does.

The sequence is built around one simple principle: fund the highest-guaranteed-return, least-flexible-later option first, and work down toward the most-flexible, lowest-guaranteed-return option last. An employer match is, structurally, as close to a guaranteed, immediate, risk-free return as exists anywhere in personal finance — money added to your account the moment you contribute, at a rate no market investment can reliably promise to match. High-interest debt sits at the other extreme of urgency for a different reason: its interest rate is also a guaranteed, immediate cost, working against you exactly the way a match works for you, and a debt carrying a double-digit interest rate is very likely costing more, with certainty, than a diversified investment portfolio is likely to earn, without certainty, over the same period. Everything else in the sequence sits between those two guaranteed numbers, ordered by a mix of tax advantage, urgency, and flexibility.

## The framework: the funding waterfall

**Step 1 — Capture the full employer match, and no more than the match, at this step.** If your employer offers any matching contribution to a 401(k) or similar plan, contribute at minimum the percentage required to receive the full match before directing money anywhere else. Skipping this step to prioritize any other option on this list is, in the overwhelming majority of real situations, leaving free money on the table in favor of a lower-certainty return elsewhere.

**Step 2 — Build or confirm a starter emergency buffer.** Before investing further, confirm you have a small cash buffer — this library's companion volume on automation covers the full account-architecture logic behind this buffer in detail — sufficient to absorb an unplanned, moderate expense without needing to sell an investment or take on debt to cover it. This isn't the full three-to-six-month buffer that a complete financial plan eventually builds toward; it's a smaller, faster first line of defense, ensuring that a car repair or a slow month at work doesn't force you to unwind an investing plan you just started.

**Step 3 — Pay down any debt carrying a genuinely high interest rate.** A specific, double-digit-interest revolving balance

— a store card carrying an interest rate in the high teens or twenties is a common real-world example, though the exact rate on any given account should always be checked directly rather than assumed — is a guaranteed cost that a diversified investment portfolio is unlikely to reliably outpace over time. Directing available money toward eliminating this kind of debt before continuing further down this funding waterfall is, mechanically, a risk-free return equal to the interest rate itself. This library's dedicated volume on debt payoff covers the full mechanics of sequencing and accelerating payoff across multiple debts, if more than one is in the picture; this step is simply about recognizing when high-interest debt should interrupt the investing waterfall rather than run in parallel with it.

**Step 4 — Max out available tax-advantaged space, in a specific order.** Once the match is captured, the buffer exists, and genuinely high-interest debt is handled or absent, direct additional savings first toward a health savings account if you have access to one and it's offered alongside a qualifying health plan, given its distinct layered tax treatment; then toward maxing your IRA contribution (Roth or traditional, per Chapter 3's framework) up to the current annual limit; then back to additional 401(k) contributions beyond the matched amount, up to that account's own current annual limit.

**Step 5 — Direct anything remaining to a taxable brokerage account.** Once available tax-advantaged space is fully used, or once a specific near-term goal calls for accessible rather than locked-up savings (a distinction covered fully in this library's companion volume on savings rate), additional investing happens in a standard taxable brokerage account, using the same fund-selection and purchasing mechanics covered in the rest of this book.

## Worked example

The dental hygienist runs her $400 a month through the waterfall. Her employer's 401(k) match requires a 4% contribution to capture fully, which, against her income, comes to $140 a month — Step 1, funded first, without exception. She confirms she already has a starter buffer of roughly one month's expenses set aside from a prior savings push, satisfying Step 2 without requiring new allocation this cycle. She has no high-interest debt, so Step 3 is a pass-through. That leaves $260 a month for Step 4: she doesn't have access to a health savings account through her current plan, so she directs the full $260 toward her Roth IRA, well within the current annual contribution limit given her income and monthly rate, and stops there for now, since she hasn't yet reached either the IRA limit or a reason to move further down the waterfall to additional 401(k) contributions or a taxable account. Her entire $400 has a specific, sequenced destination, rather than being split arbitrarily across account types by guesswork.

## A second worked example: a more complex household

A two-income household with $1,800 a month available runs the same waterfall with more moving parts. Both partners have access to an employer match, together requiring $420 a month combined to fully capture — Step 1, funded first from both incomes. They confirm their buffer is under-funded relative to Step 2's target and direct $300 a month there until it's rebuilt, planning to revisit this allocation in a few months once the buffer target is met. They're carrying a personal loan at a double-digit interest rate from a past expense, and direct an additional $400 a month toward accelerating its payoff under Step 3, on top of its required minimum, since its guaranteed interest cost outweighs the expected, uncertain return of investing that same money instead. That leaves $680 a month for Step 4, split between maxing out both partners' Roth IRA contributions up to a combined monthly-equivalent limit and directing any remainder to additional 401(k) contributions beyond the matched amount. This household's version of the waterfall looks meaningfully different from the hygienist's simpler case, not because the underlying sequence changed, but because more steps in the sequence were actively claiming a share of the available $1,800 at once.

## Common objections and how to handle them

**"What if I can't afford to fully fund even Step 1 right now?"** Contribute whatever percentage you genuinely can, even if it's below the full match threshold — partial progress on Step 1 is still better than skipping it entirely to fund a later step, given how the sequence is ordered by guaranteed return. Increase the percentage as your income allows, revisiting it at least annually, ideally alongside any raise, so the increase happens automatically rather than requiring a fresh decision each time.

**"Should I really pause investing entirely to pay off debt, per Step 3, or can I do both at once?"** For debt carrying a genuinely high interest rate, pausing additional investing beyond the captured employer match (which should almost never be skipped, even during aggressive debt payoff, given how rarely any return beats a guaranteed match) to accelerate payoff is usually the mathematically correct move, since the debt's guaranteed cost typically exceeds a diversified portfolio's expected, uncertain return. For debt carrying a moderate, single-digit interest rate — a mortgage or a low-rate auto loan, for instance — the math is closer, and running both simultaneously is a reasonable, common choice, since the guaranteed cost of that debt no longer clearly exceeds a diversified portfolio's reasonable long-run expectation.

**"Does this exact order apply to everyone, or are there real exceptions?"** The core logic — guaranteed-return items first, most-flexible items last — holds broadly, but Step 3's specific position can shift based on the exact interest rate involved, and Step 4's internal ordering can shift based on whether a health savings account is available and how its specific tax treatment compares to your other options. The waterfall is a strong, well-reasoned default, not an unbreakable law; where your specific numbers genuinely differ from the illustrative examples here, a fee-only financial advisor or tax professional can help you confirm whether an adjustment is warranted for your situation specifically.

## A note on revisiting the waterfall over time

The funding waterfall isn't a one-time decision — it's worth rerunning any time a major input changes: a raise, a new employer with a different match structure, a debt that's been paid off and freed up its monthly allocation, or a near-term goal (covered in this library's companion volume on savings rate) that newly calls for accessible rather than tax-advantaged savings. Treat this chapter's framework as a live sequence to rerun periodically, not a plan you set once at the start of your investing life and never revisit.

## Frequently misunderstood point: a low-rate mortgage isn't Step 3's target

Step 3 of this chapter's waterfall specifically targets genuinely high-interest debt, and it's worth being explicit about what doesn't belong there, since the instinct to "pay off all debt before investing anything" is common and, for a specific category of debt, usually the wrong sequencing. A mortgage carrying a modest, single-digit interest rate — and, depending on the era it was originated in, sometimes a rate well below what a diversified portfolio has reasonably been expected to return over a long horizon — doesn't carry the same guaranteed-cost urgency as the double-digit revolving debt this chapter's Step 3 is built around. Directing every available dollar toward accelerating a low-rate mortgage payoff, ahead of capturing an employer match or contributing to tax-advantaged accounts, generally sacrifices a higher, if less certain, long-run return for a lower, guaranteed one — the opposite of what Step 3's logic is built to accomplish. This isn't a claim that paying down a mortgage early is never worthwhile — some readers value the psychological certainty of an eliminated mortgage payment enough to accept the tradeoff deliberately, which is a legitimate personal choice. It's a claim that this specific tradeoff belongs to a different, more personal decision than the mechanical, largely settled sequencing this chapter's waterfall describes for genuinely high-interest debt.

## A note on windfalls

An unexpected lump sum — a bonus, a tax refund, an inheritance, the proceeds from selling something of meaningful value — doesn't require a separate decision framework distinct from this chapter's waterfall; it simply becomes a larger input run through the exact same sequence. Confirm the employer match is already being captured through your regular ongoing contribution (a windfall itself typically can't retroactively capture a missed match from earlier in the year, since the match is generally tied to payroll-deducted contributions as they happen). Then run the windfall through Steps 2 through 5 exactly as you would an ordinary monthly amount — topping off an under-funded buffer, accelerating any genuinely high-interest debt, filling remaining tax-advantaged space up to the current annual limit, and directing any remainder to a taxable account. Once the destination account is determined by the waterfall, Chapter 7's dollar-cost-averaging framework becomes directly relevant for actually investing a windfall-sized lump sum, rather than committing the entire amount in a single trade if the size of it feels uncomfortable to invest all at once.

## A note on variable and irregular income

The waterfall in this chapter assumes a specific monthly amount available to allocate, which describes most salaried readers reasonably well, but doesn't map cleanly onto genuinely variable income — freelance work, commission-based pay, seasonal employment. For a variable-income situation, the mechanical fix isn't a different waterfall; it's applying this chapter's exact sequence to whatever amount is actually available at the end of each income period, rather than waiting for a "typical" month that may not exist. This library's companion volume on savings rate covers the deeper mechanics of building a sustainable savings figure from irregular income in full; this chapter's role is simply to confirm that whatever amount that companion volume's method produces should still be run through this same funding waterfall, in the same order, regardless of how variable the underlying income happens to be from period to period.

## Common objections and how to handle them

**"What if my employer's match has a vesting schedule — does that change Step 1?"** A vesting schedule determines how much of the employer's contribution (not your own) you're entitled to keep if you leave the job before a certain point, and it doesn't change the mechanical logic of Step 1 at all — capturing the match is still close to a guaranteed, immediate return on your own contribution regardless of vesting, since your own contributed dollars are always fully yours from the moment they're deposited. A vesting schedule affects only the employer's matching portion, and even a partially vested match, if you were to leave before full vesting, is still additional value captured for free rather than value forfeited by contributing at all.

**"Should Step 4's health savings account allocation come before or after Step 1's employer match?"** Step 1 generally comes first, since an employer match is close to a universally larger effective return than a health savings account's own tax advantage, real as that advantage is. If your employer specifically matches health savings account contributions as well, treat that matched HSA contribution as part of Step 1 alongside the 401(k) match, since both represent the same category of guaranteed, immediate, employer-funded value.

## Frequently misunderstood point: the waterfall is a sequence, not an exclusive gate

A specific misreading of this chapter's framework worth correcting directly: the waterfall describes a priority order for where the next available dollar should go, not a rule that every dollar of Step 1 must be fully funded before a single dollar can ever touch Step 4. In practice, this mostly resolves itself naturally, since Step 1's employer match typically requires only a modest percentage of income, quickly satisfied, freeing the rest of an available monthly amount to flow further down the waterfall the same month. Where this distinction genuinely matters is with a larger, discrete goal like fully maxing an IRA's annual limit — you don't need to have exhausted every dollar of tax-advantaged room before ever opening a taxable account, if a genuine near-term goal, per this library's companion volume on savings rate, calls for accessible savings sooner. The waterfall orders priority, not an absolute, sequential gate that locks out every later step until the earlier one is completely exhausted.

## A note on where this chapter's waterfall sits relative to the rest of your financial plan

This chapter's waterfall assumes a specific, prior decision has already been made — that a given dollar amount is available for investing at all, distinct from what's needed for ordinary monthly expenses and the account architecture that protects them, covered in full in this library's companion volume on automation. This chapter doesn't tell you how much of your income should be set aside for investing in the first place, nor does it tell you the exact savings rate that's sustainable for your specific income and fixed costs, both covered by this library's companion volume on savings rate. What it tells you, specifically, is how to sequence whatever amount those other two questions have already determined is available. Treating this chapter's waterfall as the entire financial plan, rather than the specific piece of it that governs investment-account sequencing, is a common but avoidable overreach of what this one chapter is actually built to answer.

## A short exercise: running your own waterfall on paper

Before your next contribution, write out the five steps of this chapter's waterfall as five labeled lines on paper, and next to each one, write your own current monthly dollar amount flowing into it — including zero, honestly, for any step that currently isn't receiving anything. Total the five amounts and confirm it matches what you're actually able to set aside each month. If any step shows zero that shouldn't, per this chapter's logic — most commonly, an unclaimed employer match — that gap is the single highest-priority correction to make before your next paycheck cycle, ahead of any other adjustment to your investing plan.

## Common objections and how to handle them

**"What if my available monthly amount is small enough that it barely clears Step 1?"** A modest amount clearing only Step 1, or partially clearing it, is still a genuine, correctly sequenced start — this chapter's waterfall works identically regardless of the total amount running through it, and a small amount correctly ordered by priority is a stronger position than a larger amount split arbitrarily across steps without regard to their relative urgency. As your available amount grows, per a raise or a reduced expense, the waterfall simply continues filling downstream steps in the same order, with no need to restart or rethink the sequence itself.

**"Does this waterfall apply the same way to a couple managing money jointly?"** The underlying logic holds, applied to the household's combined available amount and combined access to employer matches, tax-advantaged space, and any household debt, rather than to each partner's income considered in isolation. Where the two partners have different employer match structures or different individual contribution limits, run Step 1 and Step 4 separately for each partner's own accounts, since an employer match and a contribution limit are both tied to the individual, not the household, even when the underlying decision about how much total money to direct toward investing is made jointly.

## A worked example: a full waterfall run with every step active at once

To show every step of this chapter's waterfall claiming a share of the same available amount simultaneously, rather than most steps sitting at zero as in the hygienist's simpler opening example, consider a warehouse manager with $1,100 available monthly. Step 1 requires $180 to capture his full employer match, funded first without exception. Step 2's starter buffer is only half-funded relative to his target, so he directs $150 a month there until it's complete, revisiting this allocation once the buffer target is reached. Step 3 identifies a personal loan carrying a 19% interest rate from a past emergency expense, and he directs $300 a month beyond the minimum payment toward accelerating its payoff, given its guaranteed cost clearly exceeds a diversified portfolio's reasonable long-run expectation. That leaves $470 for Step 4: he has access to a health savings account with no employer match offered, and directs $150 there for its own strong, independent tax treatment, then splits the remaining $320 toward maxing his Roth IRA contribution up to its monthly-equivalent share of the current annual limit. With the Roth IRA not yet fully claiming the entire $320 given his contribution room for the year, a small remainder flows to Step 5, a modest amount into a taxable brokerage account. Every single step in this chapter's five-step waterfall is active at once, in this example, each claiming exactly the priority-ordered share this chapter's framework assigns it — the more complete, more realistic version of how the waterfall usually operates once a reader’s income and obligations both exceed a beginner’s simplest starting case.

# Chapter 5 — Index Fund vs. Individual Stock

## A decision framework for a true beginner

### The situation

A schoolteacher, ready to make her first actual purchase inside her newly opened brokerage account, assumed for years that "investing in the stock market" meant picking individual companies she believed in — she has a mental shortlist of a few well-known brands she likes as a consumer. She's surprised, reading further, to find nearly every beginner-oriented resource steering her instead toward something called an index fund, a term she can define in the abstract (a fund that holds many stocks at once) but can't yet connect to a concrete reason why it would be a better starting point than simply buying shares of a company she already knows and trusts.

### The mechanics

An individual stock represents ownership in exactly one company. Its value depends entirely on that one company's performance, competitive position, management decisions, and broader industry conditions — a concentrated bet, for better or worse, on a single outcome. An index fund, by contrast, is a fund — either structured as a mutual fund or as an exchange-traded fund — built to hold a broad basket of stocks matching a specific market index, most commonly something like the S&P; 500, an index of roughly five hundred large publicly traded U.S. companies across essentially every major industry. Buying one share of a fund tracking that index gives you simultaneous, proportional ownership across all five hundred companies inside it, in a single purchase, at a cost far lower than buying five hundred individual positions yourself.

The case for index funds as a sensible default, particularly for a beginner, rests on a body of real, published research and a set of well-documented historical patterns, not on a marketing claim. S&P; Dow Jones Indices publishes an ongoing research report called the SPIVA Scorecard (SPIVA stands for S&P; Indices Versus Active), which has consistently found, across long measurement periods, that a majority of actively managed funds — funds where a manager is actively picking individual stocks in an attempt to beat the market — underperform their relevant benchmark index over extended time horizons, after accounting for fees. This isn't a claim that no actively managed fund or individual investor ever outperforms an index; some clearly do, in any given period. It's a claim about the odds, and the odds, according to this ongoing, publicly available research, consistently favor the low-cost index approach over a long horizon for most investors.

The index fund itself has a specific, documented origin worth knowing. John Bogle, founder of Vanguard, created the first index mutual fund available to individual investors in 1976, built on the argument — laid out at length in his own published writing, including his book *Common Sense on Mutual Funds* — that most investors would be better served matching the market's return at minimal cost than paying higher fees in an attempt to beat it, an attempt that, per the SPIVA research above, more often fails than succeeds after fees are accounted for. Economist Burton Malkiel made a related, independently developed case in his long-running book *A Random Walk Down Wall Street*, arguing that stock price movements are difficult enough to predict consistently that a broad, low-cost, diversified approach tends to outperform an attempt at individual stock-picking for most ordinary investors over time.

None of this means individual stocks are inherently a mistake to own. It means concentrated ownership in a single company carries a level of risk — tied to that one company's specific fortunes — that a broad index fund, by its structural design, diversifies away. The decision in front of a beginner isn't "index fund or individual stock" as a permanent, exclusive choice; it's "what role does each play, and in what proportion, given how much risk concentration I actually want to carry."

## The framework: core and explore

A useful, widely used structure for thinking about this decision splits a portfolio into two conceptual pieces, applied in whatever proportion fits your own comfort with risk.

**The core** is the portion of your investments built for reliable, long-horizon growth with broad diversification — typically one or more low-cost index funds or ETFs covering a wide swath of the market, the kind of holding this chapter's mechanics section has been describing throughout. For a true beginner, the reasonable default is to make this the large majority of a portfolio, since it's the piece doing the actual long-term compounding work with the least concentrated risk.

**The explore** portion, if you choose to have one at all, is a smaller allocation set aside specifically for individual stock selection, sector-specific funds, or other more concentrated bets — money you're comfortable seeing underperform, or even lose meaningfully, without it derailing your broader financial goals, since concentrated positions carry real volatility that a diversified core is specifically designed to avoid.

A commonly used starting ratio for a beginner who wants some exposure to individual stock-picking without meaningfully compromising the core's diversification benefit is roughly 90% core, 10% explore, adjusted up or down based on your own risk tolerance and how much you genuinely want to spend time researching individual companies. There's no single correct ratio — the framework's value is in the deliberate split itself, made consciously in advance, rather than letting individual stock purchases creep into a portfolio unplanned and unbounded.

## Worked example

The schoolteacher from this chapter's opening applies the core-and-explore framework to her first year of investing. She directs 90% of her monthly contribution into a single broad market index fund — chosen using Chapter 2's brokerage scorecard and confirmed to carry a low expense ratio using Chapter 6's method — as her core holding, and sets aside the remaining 10% for two individual stocks in companies she's genuinely familiar with as a consumer and has done some basic research into. She frames this 10% explicitly, in her own plan, as money she's comfortable seeing underperform or decline without changing her broader retirement timeline, distinct from her core holding, which she's built to actually count on. A year later, one of her two individual stock picks has done well and one has lagged behind her core index fund's performance — a genuinely common outcome for concentrated single-stock bets — but because the explore allocation was deliberately capped at 10% from the start, neither outcome meaningfully changed her overall trajectory, which is exactly what the framework is designed to ensure.

## Common objections and how to handle them

**"If index funds usually win, why would anyone bother with individual stocks at all?"** Some investors genuinely enjoy researching individual companies as an engaged, active hobby, and are willing to accept the added risk and the research time as the cost of that engagement — a legitimate reason, as long as it's bounded, per this chapter's framework, rather than allowed to dominate a portfolio without a deliberate decision to let it. Others hold a specific, informed conviction about a particular company or sector and choose to size a position accordingly, within an explore allocation. Neither reason contradicts the broader research on average outcomes — it simply means an individual investor is making a deliberate, bounded, informed tradeoff rather than defaulting into concentration by accident.

**"Isn't picking a single index fund still a form of picking, the same as picking a stock?"** Mechanically, yes — you are choosing a specific fund. But the risk profile is fundamentally different: a broad index fund's fortunes are tied to hundreds of companies across many industries simultaneously, meaning no single company's failure meaningfully threatens the fund's overall value, while a single stock's fortunes are tied entirely to one company's outcome. The "picking" involved in choosing a broad index fund is a decision about cost and breadth of exposure, covered in Chapter 6; the "picking" involved in choosing a single stock is a decision about a specific company's future, a fundamentally different and higher-risk kind of judgment call.

**"What about sector-specific or thematic funds — do those count as core or explore?"** A fund concentrated in a single sector or theme, even if it holds many companies within that sector, still carries more concentrated risk than a truly broad market index fund, since an entire sector can move together in ways an individual company's problems typically don't. Treat a sector-specific or thematic fund as closer to the explore category than the core category for the purposes of this chapter's framework, unless you have a specific, informed reason to treat a given sector as core to your particular financial plan.

## A note on what "the market" actually refers to

Beginners occasionally hear "invest in the market" and picture something more mysterious or exclusive than it actually is. A broad market index fund is, in mechanical terms, simply a basket of ownership stakes in a wide cross-section of real, operating businesses — the same kind of companies whose products and services show up in ordinary daily life — pooled together and divided into shares anyone can buy through an ordinary brokerage account. There's no separate, more sophisticated "market" that professional or wealthy investors access and beginners don't; the core holding this chapter recommends is available, at the same price and the same terms, to anyone with a brokerage account and a few dollars to invest, regardless of experience level.

## A short exercise before your first purchase

Before making your first purchase, write down, honestly, what proportion of your investable money you'd genuinely be comfortable seeing concentrated in a small number of individual companies rather than spread broadly — not an aspirational number, but a real one, tested against how you'd actually feel watching a single holding decline by a meaningful percentage in a bad month. Use that honest number as your explore allocation ceiling, and direct the remainder to a core index holding. If your honest answer is zero, that's a completely legitimate outcome of this exercise, not a failure to engage with individual stock-picking — a 100% core portfolio, built entirely from low-cost, broadly diversified index funds, is a genuinely sound, widely used approach on its own.

## Frequently misunderstood point: diversified isn't the same as risk-free

A broad index fund removes the concentrated, single-company risk that comes with owning one stock, but it doesn't remove market risk itself — the value of a broad market index fund still moves up and down with the overall market, sometimes sharply, and a beginner who mistakes "diversified" for "guaranteed to grow steadily" is setting up for a jarring first experience with an ordinary market decline. The specific risk an index fund is built to diversify away is company-specific risk: the chance that one business's individual failure — a scandal, a bankruptcy, a lost lawsuit — wipes out a concentrated position. It does nothing to diversify away broad, market-wide risk, since by definition it's designed to move with the market rather than around it. Understanding this distinction in advance is worth more than it might seem in the moment you open your first account; it's the difference between correctly expecting an ordinary decline as a normal, survivable feature of investing and mistaking it for a sign that something has gone specifically wrong with your particular choice of fund.

## A note on dividend reinvestment, mechanically

Many funds and individual stocks periodically pay a dividend — a cash distribution to shareholders, generally funded from a company's or fund's underlying profits. Left as cash, a dividend simply adds to your account's cash balance, subject to the same "deposited but not invested" issue Chapter 1 flagged as the most common beginner mistake. Most brokerages offer a dividend reinvestment feature — commonly abbreviated DRIP — that automatically uses any dividend received to purchase additional shares (including fractional shares) of the same holding that paid it, the moment the dividend lands, with no manual action required. For a long-horizon core holding, turning this feature on is a small, one-time setting that keeps every dollar received continuously working rather than sitting idle in cash between your regular contribution dates — confirm it's enabled for your core holding specifically, since some brokerages set it as an opt-in rather than a default.

## A second worked example: choosing a fully diversified portfolio with no explore allocation

A different first-time investor, working through this same chapter, decides honestly that she has no interest in researching individual companies and would rather her entire portfolio track the broad market with no concentrated positions at all. She directs 100% of her contributions to a single broad market index fund, skipping the explore allocation entirely — a fully legitimate application of this chapter's framework, since the core-and-explore split is a tool for those who want some individual-stock exposure, not a requirement that everyone carry one. A year later, her portfolio's performance simply tracks the broad index she chose, with no single company's individual result meaningfully swinging her outcome in either direction — precisely the tradeoff she deliberately chose, and precisely what the framework is built to let her choose deliberately rather than by default.

## A note on bonds as a second core building block

This chapter has focused on the stock-versus-individual-stock decision within the equity portion of a portfolio, but a complete core holding, for most investors, isn't 100% stocks — it typically includes some allocation to bonds as well, a fundamentally different kind of security representing a loan to a government or corporation rather than ownership in a company, generally carrying lower expected long-run return alongside lower typical volatility. A broad bond index fund functions mechanically the same way a broad stock index fund does — a single fund holding a diversified basket, purchased the same way, carrying its own expense ratio worth checking using Chapter 6's framework. The specific ratio between stocks and bonds in a core holding is a function of how much volatility an investor is comfortable with and how far off their investing goal sits in time, a genuinely individual judgment call that a beginner-focused mechanics book can responsibly describe as a real, important decision without prescribing a single universal ratio — a common practitioner rule of thumb ties bond allocation loosely to age or time horizon, with a higher bond percentage as a goal approaches, though the specific number is a matter of individual risk tolerance best refined with a fee-only financial advisor if the decision feels genuinely uncertain.

## Common objections and how to handle them

**"What about funds that hold both stocks and bonds together in one product?"** These exist, commonly as target-date funds (which automatically shift their stock-to-bond ratio as a target year, usually a retirement year, approaches) or as fixed-allocation balanced funds. Either can serve as a single, simplified stand-in for the entire core holding this chapter describes, appropriate for an investor who wants the diversification benefit of a stock-and-bond mix without manually managing the ratio themselves — the tradeoff, as with any bundled product, is confirming its expense ratio using Chapter 6's framework, since convenience and cost aren't always aligned.

**"Is it ever reasonable to have more than 10% in the explore allocation?"** The 90/10 split offered earlier in this chapter is a common, reasonable starting point, not a fixed ceiling — an investor with a longer time horizon, a higher genuine tolerance for volatility, and a specific, informed interest in individual company research can reasonably choose a larger explore allocation, provided the choice is made deliberately using this chapter's honest self-assessment exercise rather than by allowing individual purchases to creep upward unplanned over time.

## A note on how many funds a core holding actually needs

A beginner sometimes assumes a properly diversified core requires assembling several different funds — a large-company fund, a small-company fund, an international fund, and so on — layered together deliberately. This is a genuinely valid, more granular approach some investors prefer, but it isn't a requirement, and it's worth saying plainly that a single, sufficiently broad fund can serve as a complete core holding on its own. A fund tracking a genuinely broad, all-market index, or a fund specifically constructed to hold a globally diversified mix of stocks in one product, already provides the diversification benefit this book's Chapter 5 has been describing throughout, without requiring an investor to separately select and maintain the correct proportions across several individual funds themselves. Starting with one broad, low-cost core fund is a completely sufficient, legitimate choice for a first year of investing, and splitting that core into more granular pieces later, once you have a specific, informed reason to do so, remains entirely available whenever you're ready for it.

## A note on international exposure specifically

A specific question that comes up often enough to address directly: should a beginner's core holding include exposure to companies outside their home country, or is a domestic-only broad index sufficient? Both are legitimate, widely used approaches, and reasonable, informed investors land on different answers. A domestic broad-market index fund, for a U.S. investor, already provides substantial diversification across hundreds of large companies with significant international revenue exposure embedded within them, even without holding any foreign-domiciled stock directly. A globally diversified fund, or a domestic fund paired with a separate international index fund, adds direct exposure to companies headquartered and primarily operating outside the investor's home country, which some investors deliberately add specifically to avoid over-concentrating in a single country's economic and market cycle. Neither choice is a mistake within this chapter's framework — it's a genuine, individual judgment call about how broad "broad" should be for your specific core holding, worth a deliberate decision rather than defaulting into either option without having considered the other.

# Chapter 6 — Reading an Expense Ratio

## Why a small number is a big deal

### The situation

An electrician comparing two broad market index funds, both tracking essentially the same underlying index and holding essentially the same companies, notices they're priced differently per share and assumes the cheaper per-share price is the better deal — a natural but mistaken instinct, since share price and cost of ownership are two entirely different numbers. Buried in each fund's fact sheet, in a line he almost skipped past, is a number labeled "expense ratio" — 0.03% for one fund, 0.75% for the other. Both numbers look small enough to seem irrelevant at first glance, and he has no immediate sense of why a difference of roughly seven-tenths of one percent would be worth paying attention to at all.

### The mechanics

An expense ratio is the annual fee a fund charges to cover its own operating costs, expressed as a percentage of the total money you have invested in it. It isn't billed to you as a separate charge you'll notice on a statement — it's deducted automatically and continuously from the fund's returns, which means a fund charging a 0.75% expense ratio simply delivers you a return 0.75 percentage points lower, every year, than the exact same holdings would have delivered at zero cost. This invisibility is precisely why it's easy to underweight: there's no bill to open, no line item to react to, just a slightly smaller number showing up in your account balance than would otherwise have been there, year after year, without a single moment that draws attention to it.

The reason a difference that looks small on paper matters so much comes down to how compounding works. Money isn't just growing on your original contribution each year — it's growing on all the accumulated prior growth as well, and a fee applied every single year is a fee applied to an ever-larger base as your account grows over a multi-decade investing horizon. A 0.75% annual drag doesn't just cost you 0.75% of your final balance; it costs you 0.75% of every year's growth, compounded across every remaining year the money stays invested, which is a meaningfully larger cumulative effect than the small annual percentage suggests on its own.

Here's the math made concrete, using a purely illustrative example, not a guaranteed or historical return figure: assume $10,000 invested today, left untouched for 30 years, growing at an assumed 7% average annual return before fees — an illustrative planning assumption used widely in this library and elsewhere, not a promise about actual future market performance. At a 0.03% expense ratio, essentially the entire 7% return compounds for 30 years, growing that $10,000 to a little over $76,000. At a 0.75% expense ratio, the effective compounding rate drops to roughly 6.25%, growing the same $10,000 over the same 30 years to a little under $62,000. The difference — roughly $14,000, on a single $10,000 initial investment, from a fee difference that looked like less than one percentage point — is the entire lesson of this chapter made visible in a single number. Run across a full career's worth of ongoing contributions rather than a single lump sum, the cumulative cost of an elevated expense ratio grows substantially larger still.

Broad market index funds and ETFs, specifically, have become available at extremely low expense ratios industry-wide — commonly a few hundredths of one percent for the largest, most broadly diversified options — because tracking an index mechanically requires little active management, and competition among major providers has pushed pricing on these products down substantially over time. Actively managed funds, where a manager or team is making ongoing decisions about which securities to hold, typically charge meaningfully more, often somewhere in the range of half a percent to well over one percent annually, to cover the cost of that active management — a cost that, per Chapter 5's discussion of the SPIVA research, doesn't reliably translate into outperformance sufficient to justify it for most investors over long periods.

## The framework: finding and evaluating an expense ratio

**Step 1 — Locate the expense ratio before buying anything, not after.** It's published in a fund's prospectus and fact sheet, both freely available on the fund provider's website, and is typically also displayed directly on your brokerage's own fund research page when you search a ticker. Don't assume — look it up directly for the specific fund you're considering, every time, since it varies fund to fund even among funds that look similar on the surface.

**Step 2 — Compare it against a reasonable benchmark for that fund's category.** A broad market index fund or ETF should generally carry an expense ratio in the low hundredths of a percent; if a fund marketed as a broad index tracker carries a notably higher fee than comparable options, that's worth investigating specifically before buying, since it may indicate additional active management, a narrower or more specialized underlying index, or simply a less competitively priced provider.

**Step 3 — Check for other fees beyond the expense ratio.** Some mutual funds carry a "load" — a sales charge applied when you buy or sell shares, on top of the ongoing expense ratio, historically more common with funds sold through a commission-based advisor. Some funds also carry a smaller "12b-1 fee," a marketing and distribution cost baked into the expense ratio figure itself. Confirm you're looking at the fund's total, all-in annual cost, not just a headline number that omits an additional charge disclosed elsewhere in the fact sheet.

**Step 4 — Run the compounding math on your own numbers before dismissing a fee difference as too small to matter.** Use this chapter's illustrative calculation as a template, substituting your own expected contribution amount and time horizon, to see the actual dollar impact of a specific fee difference on your specific plan, rather than relying on intuition about a small-looking percentage.

## Worked example

The electrician from this chapter's opening runs the two funds he was comparing through this framework. Both track the same broad index and hold effectively the same underlying companies, confirming that the meaningfully different expense ratios aren't reflecting a genuine difference in what he'd actually own. He finds no sales load on either fund, so the expense ratio figures represent the real, full comparison. Using this chapter's illustrative 30-year compounding calculation, adjusted to his own planned $15,000 initial investment, he estimates the higher-fee fund would cost him several thousand dollars more over three decades than the lower-fee fund, for functionally identical underlying exposure. He selects the lower-cost fund, not because the higher-cost one was fraudulent or poorly built, but because paying meaningfully more for functionally identical exposure has no offsetting benefit he can identify.

## Common objections and how to handle them

**"Doesn't a higher expense ratio sometimes mean better management or better results?"** For an actively managed fund, that's the underlying premise the higher fee is meant to justify — a skilled manager delivering returns worth the extra cost. Per the SPIVA research discussed in Chapter 5, this premise holds for some funds in some periods, but fails to hold, on average, across the majority of actively managed funds over long horizons, after fees are accounted for. For a broad index fund specifically, where the entire premise is mechanically matching an index rather than beating it, there's no plausible mechanism by which a higher expense ratio should correlate with better results at all — the index is the index, and a fund tracking it well should aim to replicate its performance as closely and cheaply as possible, not deviate from it.

**"Is a 0.03% difference really worth switching funds over if I already own the more expensive one?"** Run the compounding math on your own actual balance and time horizon before deciding, since the answer depends heavily on how much is invested and how long it has left to grow. For a modest, recently opened balance, the cumulative difference may be small enough that the decision comes down to convenience. For a substantial balance with decades remaining, this chapter's math suggests the difference is usually worth acting on — and switching, within a tax-advantaged account, typically carries no tax consequence at all, making it a low-cost decision to correct once identified.

**"What if the lower-cost fund I found doesn't track exactly the same index as a fund I already prefer?"** This is a legitimate reason for a fee difference to exist and to matter less than the raw numbers suggest — two funds tracking genuinely different indices, with different composition and different risk profiles, aren't a clean apples-to-apples comparison regardless of their expense ratios. Confirm you're comparing funds tracking the same or a very similar underlying index before treating a fee gap as pure, uncompensated cost.

## A short exercise before your next purchase

For any fund you're currently considering, or already own, look up its expense ratio directly on the fund provider's website or your brokerage's fund research page, and write it down next to a comparable broad-index alternative's expense ratio. If a meaningful gap exists between the two for functionally similar exposure, run this chapter's compounding calculation using your own actual or planned investment amount and time horizon, and let the resulting dollar figure — not the small-looking percentage on its own — inform your decision.

## Frequently misunderstood point: the lowest expense ratio isn't automatically the best choice

This chapter has made a sustained case for taking expense ratio seriously, and it's worth closing with the boundary of that case, so it doesn't get overapplied. Expense ratio is a critical variable for comparing two funds that hold essentially the same thing — two broad market index funds tracking the same underlying index, for instance, where a lower fee is close to a straightforward improvement with no offsetting tradeoff. It's a much less decisive variable when comparing two funds that hold genuinely different things, since a fund's actual holdings and how well it tracks its stated index (a concept called tracking error, referring to how closely a fund's actual return matches the index it's meant to follow) matter as much as, or more than, a small fee difference once the underlying exposure itself isn't a clean match. The discipline this chapter is teaching is to compare expense ratios among genuinely comparable funds, not to treat the single lowest expense ratio on the market, regardless of what the fund actually holds, as an automatic winner.

## A note on account-level and transaction-level fees beyond the fund itself

Separate from any individual fund's expense ratio, a small number of other account-level costs are worth checking for once, at account opening, since they're easy to overlook amid the fund-level comparison this chapter has focused on. Some brokerages charge a transaction fee specifically for buying certain mutual funds from outside providers, distinct from the fund's own expense ratio — generally avoidable by sticking to a brokerage's own no-transaction-fee fund lineup, confirmed as part of Chapter 2's brokerage scorecard. A small number of brokerages also charge an account maintenance fee on certain account types, sometimes waived once a minimum balance or a recurring deposit is established — worth confirming directly rather than assuming it doesn't apply. None of these costs are as large or as consequential over time as an elevated expense ratio compounding across decades, but confirming they don't apply to your specific account, once, at the start, closes off a small, avoidable leak alongside the much larger one this chapter's main framework addresses.

## A note on where the illustrative compounding math in this chapter came from

The specific dollar figures used earlier in this chapter's compounding calculation follow standard, widely available future-value-of-a-lump-sum arithmetic — the same formula taught in any introductory finance course, not a proprietary calculation unique to this book. Readers wanting to run the exact math on their own specific numbers, rather than trusting this chapter's illustrative figures, can use any reputable, freely available compound-interest or fee-impact calculator, including tools published directly by financial regulators for exactly this purpose, referenced further in this book's closing Notes & Further Reading section. The point of running your own numbers isn't to second-guess the mechanism described in this chapter — the mechanism is simple, verifiable arithmetic — but to see the actual dollar impact on your own specific contribution amount and time horizon, which will differ from this chapter's $10,000, 30-year illustration in ways that matter to your own decision.

## Common objections and how to handle them

**"Does expense ratio matter as much for a shorter time horizon?"** The compounding effect described in this chapter grows more pronounced the longer money stays invested, which means a fee difference matters proportionally less for a genuinely short-horizon goal — a few years rather than a few decades. It doesn't stop mattering entirely even on a shorter horizon, since an elevated fee still directly reduces return in any single year, but the dramatic, decades-long compounding gap this chapter's worked example demonstrates is specifically a long-horizon phenomenon, worth calibrating your own concern about a given fee difference against your own actual time horizon for that specific holding.

**"Is there ever a good reason to pay a higher expense ratio deliberately?"** Yes, in specific, narrow cases — a fund offering genuinely differentiated exposure unavailable at lower cost elsewhere (a specific, narrow strategy or asset class with no low-cost broad alternative), or an actively managed fund with a long, well-documented track record an investor has specifically researched and decided to pay for. For the broad, diversified core holding this book's framework centers on, these exceptions rarely apply, since broad market exposure is now available at minimal cost from multiple major providers, leaving little genuine justification for paying meaningfully more for the same underlying exposure.

## A note on how expense ratios have changed over time

It's worth knowing, as general context rather than a specific number to memorize, that expense ratios on broad index funds have declined substantially over the decades since Bogle's original 1976 index fund launched, driven by competition among major fund providers and the sheer scale that broad index funds have achieved as more investors have adopted them. This matters for a beginner mainly as reassurance: a genuinely low-cost, broad index option is not a rare or hard-to-find product requiring special access — it's become the industry-standard baseline across nearly every major brokerage, precisely because of the competitive pressure this chapter's underlying logic has exerted across the entire fund industry over an extended period. The specific numbers will keep changing; the direction, historically, has been consistently favorable to investors who understand what to look for.

## A short exercise: pricing your own current holdings

If you already own any fund at all, before reading further into this book, look up its expense ratio right now and write down the actual annual dollar cost it represents against your current balance — simply your balance multiplied by the expense ratio percentage. Seeing this as a concrete dollar figure, rather than an abstract percentage, tends to sharpen the decision considerably more than the percentage alone does. If the resulting number feels larger than expected, revisit Chapter 2's brokerage scorecard and this chapter's framework together, and confirm whether a lower-cost, comparably diversified alternative exists for the same underlying exposure — a switch that, inside a tax-advantaged account, generally carries no cost of its own beyond the small effort of making it.

## Common objections and how to handle them

**"How do I compare an expense ratio across a mutual fund version and an ETF version of what's essentially the same underlying index?"** Many major fund providers offer both a mutual fund and an ETF share class tracking the identical underlying index, and it's genuinely common for the two to carry different expense ratios, sometimes with the ETF version priced lower. Compare them directly using this chapter's framework exactly as you would any two distinct funds — the "mutual fund versus ETF" distinction affects trading mechanics per Chapter 8, not whether this chapter's cost comparison applies, which it does identically to both structures.

**"If I already own a higher-cost fund inside a taxable account, is switching still worth the tax cost of selling?"** This requires weighing this chapter's compounding math against the specific capital gains tax you'd trigger by selling an appreciated position, a genuinely case-by-case calculation depending on how large the embedded gain is and your own tax rate. For a modest embedded gain, switching to a meaningfully lower-cost comparable fund is often still worth the one-time tax cost, given how the fee savings compound going forward; for a large embedded gain built up over many years, the math shifts, and holding the existing position while directing all new contributions to the lower-cost alternative — rather than selling the whole position outright — is often the more sensible middle path, worth confirming against your own specific numbers, ideally with a tax professional if the embedded gain is substantial.

## A note on how to talk about expense ratios with someone else who's just starting out

If you've worked through this chapter and later find yourself explaining expense ratios to a friend, a sibling, or a coworker who's just starting their own investing journey, the single most effective explanation isn't the percentage itself — it's this chapter's dollar-figure translation, run on a number that means something to them specifically. Telling someone "a 0.75% fee sounds small" rarely lands with any real weight. Telling them "on your specific $20,000 balance, that's roughly $150 a year, every year, for as long as you hold it, compounding against you the whole time" tends to land immediately, because it converts an abstract percentage into the same kind of concrete number they already use to evaluate any other recurring cost in their life — a subscription, a monthly bill, a recurring fee they'd notice and question anywhere else. This chapter's entire teaching method is built around that same translation, and it's worth carrying forward any time this topic comes up outside the pages of this book.

# Chapter 7 — Dollar-Cost Averaging

## The actual mechanics and a real schedule

## The situation

A research technician has $6,000 saved and ready to invest, has cleared every prior chapter's vocabulary and account-setup hurdles, and is now frozen by a different kind of fear entirely: the fear of investing the whole amount today and watching the market decline the following week. She's heard the phrase "dollar-cost averaging" used as a solution to this fear but doesn't understand it mechanically beyond a vague sense that it means "investing a little at a time instead of all at once."

## The mechanics

Dollar-cost averaging (DCA) is the practice of investing a fixed dollar amount at regular, predetermined intervals, regardless of what the price happens to be doing at each interval, rather than investing a lump sum all at once. Because the dollar amount is fixed and the price varies, this mechanically results in buying more shares when the price is lower and fewer shares when the price is higher, which averages your effective cost per share over the whole schedule rather than locking in a single purchase price on a single day.

It's worth being precise and honest about what DCA does and doesn't accomplish, because it's sometimes oversold as a strategy that improves returns, which isn't quite what the actual research shows. Vanguard published a widely cited 2012 research paper directly comparing dollar-cost averaging against investing a lump sum immediately, using historical market data across multiple markets and multi-decade periods. The finding was that investing the full lump sum immediately outperformed a dollar-cost-averaged schedule roughly two-thirds of the time historically, essentially because markets have trended upward over most extended historical periods, and money invested sooner has, on average, more time to participate in that growth than money deliberately held back and drip-fed in over months. This is a real, important finding, and it means DCA isn't a mathematical trick that reliably beats a lump sum.

What DCA does provide, and what the same body of research acknowledges directly, is a genuine reduction in regret risk — the specific, real possibility of investing a large lump sum immediately before a significant, sharp decline, and the psychological and behavioral cost of that outcome, which can be severe enough to derail an investing plan entirely if it causes someone to panic and sell at a loss, or to avoid investing again for years afterward out of a bad experience. For someone whose genuine alternative to a DCA schedule is not investing the lump sum at all — sitting in cash indefinitely out of fear, rather than actually committing to a lump sum — a DCA schedule that gets the money invested steadily over a defined period is a substantially better outcome than the alternative of paralysis, even though it isn't mathematically favored over an immediate lump sum for someone who could genuinely tolerate investing all at once without an elevated risk of panic-selling into a decline.

The practical takeaway, held honestly against the actual research rather than a simplified version of it: if you can genuinely tolerate the emotional experience of investing a lump sum immediately and holding through whatever the market does next, the research modestly favors doing exactly that. If the honest alternative to a DCA schedule is indefinite inaction driven by fear, a defined, time-bound DCA schedule that gets the money working is the better real-world choice, since the cost of prolonged inaction — money sitting uninvested, earning little, for months or years — is a real, quantifiable cost of its own, not a neutral, risk-free default.

## The framework: building a real DCA schedule

**Step 1 — Decide the total amount and be specific about it.** A vague intention to "invest gradually" without a defined total and endpoint tends to drift into indefinite postponement, defeating the entire purpose. Name the exact dollar amount you're spreading out.

**Step 2 — Choose an interval.** Common choices are weekly, biweekly, or monthly — the specific interval matters less than picking one and sticking to it consistently. A monthly interval is often the simplest to align with paycheck timing and to automate cleanly through a brokerage's recurring purchase feature, covered in Chapter 2's brokerage-selection criteria.

**Step 3 — Choose a duration, and keep it relatively short rather than indefinite.** A schedule stretched across three to twelve months is a common, reasonable range for spreading out a specific lump sum; stretching much beyond that starts to meaningfully increase the amount of time the remaining, not-yet-invested portion sits in cash, missing out on potential growth for longer than the regret-reduction benefit typically justifies. There's no single correct duration — the goal is picking one deliberately, in advance, rather than letting the schedule extend indefinitely out of ongoing hesitation.

**Step 4 — Automate it.** Set up a recurring purchase for the fixed dollar amount at the chosen interval directly through your brokerage, using the automatic recurring-purchase feature confirmed as available during Chapter 2's brokerage selection. Automating this step removes the need to make a fresh, emotionally loaded decision at every single interval, which is precisely the discipline DCA is meant to provide in the first place — a schedule you have to manually execute each time reintroduces the exact hesitation the schedule was built to route around.

**Step 5 — Know your transition point in advance.** Once the lump sum is fully invested according to the schedule, transition to investing new, ongoing contributions (from your regular paycheck, for instance) as they arrive, rather than continuing to artificially stretch out purchases beyond the original lump sum's schedule. At that point, you're no longer dollar-cost-averaging a lump sum — you're simply investing new money as it comes in, which is the ordinary, steady-state version of investing this entire book has been building toward.

## Worked example

The research technician from this chapter's opening builds a schedule for her $6,000: a six-month duration, $1,000 invested on the first of each month, automated through her brokerage's recurring purchase feature into the core index fund she selected using Chapter 5's framework. Six months later, the full $6,000 is invested, having bought more shares during two months where the fund's price dipped and fewer shares during the months it climbed, averaging her effective cost per share across the full period rather than locking in a single day's price. From that point forward, she transitions to investing $400 a month from her ongoing paycheck — the amount her Chapter 4 funding waterfall allocated to her taxable account after her tax-advantaged contributions — as a simple, steady, ongoing contribution, no longer following a DCA schedule in any meaningful sense, since there's no longer a lump sum being spread out, just new income being invested as it arrives.

## A second worked example: a shorter, more aggressive schedule

Someone with a $12,000 lump sum and a higher tolerance for near-term price movement chooses a three-month schedule instead, investing $4,000 a month, reasoning that a longer schedule would leave too much of the total sitting in cash for too long relative to their comfort with short-term volatility. This is a legitimate, personal calibration of Step 3 — a shorter schedule gets money invested faster, which the underlying research modestly favors, at the cost of somewhat less protection against the specific bad-timing scenario a longer schedule spreads risk across. Neither this three-month schedule nor the technician's six-month schedule is objectively correct; both are reasonable applications of the same framework, calibrated to a different personal comfort level with the tradeoff this chapter has described honestly throughout.

## Common objections and how to handle them

**"If lump-sum investing usually wins, why would I ever choose DCA at all?"** Because the honest, realistic alternative for many people isn't a confident lump sum — it's indefinite postponement driven by fear of bad timing. Compared against that real alternative, not against an idealized version of yourself who could invest a lump sum without hesitation, a defined DCA schedule is very often the better actual choice, since it guarantees the money gets invested within a bounded, known period rather than sitting in cash indefinitely.

**"What if the market drops significantly partway through my DCA schedule?"** This is, mechanically, DCA doing exactly what it's designed to do — a drop partway through the schedule means your remaining scheduled purchases buy more shares at the lower price than they would have otherwise, which is the averaging mechanism working as intended, not a sign the schedule has failed. Resist the urge to pause or abandon the schedule specifically because of a decline; interrupting it defeats the purpose and reintroduces exactly the timing risk the schedule exists to spread out.

**"Should I use DCA for my ongoing, regular paycheck contributions too, not just a lump sum?"** Regular contributions from an ongoing paycheck are, by their nature, already a form of steady, interval-based investing, since new money arrives and gets invested on a recurring schedule automatically — this is functionally the same mechanism as DCA, just without a defined lump sum or endpoint, since paycheck income itself has no natural stopping point. The specific, bounded DCA schedule from this chapter's framework applies most directly to a one-time lump sum; ongoing paycheck-driven contributions are already living in the steady-state version of the same underlying principle.

## A short exercise before investing a lump sum

If you have a lump sum ready to invest, write down the four inputs from this chapter's framework explicitly before doing anything else: the total amount, the interval, the duration, and the specific automated mechanism you'll use to execute it. Set the automation up before the first scheduled purchase date, not on the date itself, so the first purchase happens without requiring a fresh, in-the-moment decision — the entire value of this framework depends on removing exactly that decision from your hands once the schedule is set.

## Frequently misunderstood point: DCA is not market timing, and isn't trying to be

It's worth being precise about what dollar-cost averaging is not, since it's occasionally confused with a more active, prediction-based strategy it has nothing to do with. Market timing refers to an attempt to predict short-term market movements and buy or sell based on that prediction — selling before an anticipated decline, buying before an anticipated rally. Dollar-cost averaging makes no prediction whatsoever about what the market will do next; it invests a fixed amount on a fixed schedule regardless of what happens to the price, which is precisely the opposite of trying to time anything. A DCA schedule that happens to buy more shares during a decline isn't "correctly timing" that decline — it's simply following a predetermined rule that happens to buy more when the price is lower, by mechanical construction, not by predictive skill. Keeping this distinction clear matters practically: if the schedule tempts you to start pausing or accelerating purchases based on a hunch about where the market is headed next, you've quietly stopped doing dollar-cost averaging and started attempting market timing instead, which is a fundamentally different, and far less reliable, activity.

## A note on automating a schedule across more than one fund at once

Everything in this chapter's framework has described a schedule funding a single core holding, but the same mechanics extend cleanly to a schedule split across more than one fund — for instance, a lump sum being dollar-cost-averaged into a broad stock index fund and a bond index fund simultaneously, in a fixed ratio, to build a specific target allocation (the same target allocation Chapter 9's rebalancing framework is built to maintain going forward) from the very first purchase rather than starting concentrated in a single fund and rebalancing into a target mix later. Most brokerage recurring-purchase tools support scheduling more than one automated purchase on the same recurring date, simply set up as separate recurring orders for each fund, sized to reflect your intended split of the total periodic amount. There's no meaningful mechanical difference between this and the single-fund version described earlier in this chapter — it's the same framework, applied to more than one destination at once.

## Common objections and how to handle them

**"What if I get a second, larger lump sum partway through an existing DCA schedule?"** Treat it as a decision point rather than automatically folding it into the existing schedule. Depending on the size of the new amount and your own comfort level, a reasonable approach is either extending the current schedule's per-interval amount to absorb it, or, more simply, treating the new sum as its own independent schedule running in parallel, using Step 1 through Step 4 fresh for that specific amount. Either is legitimate; what matters is a deliberate choice rather than an unplanned, ad hoc adjustment to an already-running schedule.

**"Should I pause my DCA schedule if I lose confidence partway through?"** This is the exact moment this chapter's framework is built to protect against — a schedule interrupted midway based on a change in feeling, rather than a change in the underlying plan, reintroduces the timing risk the schedule exists to spread out in the first place. If your confidence in the specific fund you chose has genuinely changed based on new, substantive information, that's a fund-selection question to revisit using Chapter 5's framework, distinct from the DCA schedule's execution, which is built to run on autopilot specifically so that ordinary, expected fluctuations in confidence don't interrupt it.

**"Is there a minimum lump sum size below which a DCA schedule doesn't make sense?"** For a genuinely small amount — a few hundred dollars, for instance — the regret-risk this chapter's framework is designed to reduce is proportionally smaller too, and a single lump-sum purchase, per the research discussed in this chapter's mechanics section, is often simply the more straightforward choice. DCA schedules earn their keep most clearly on a lump sum large enough that the emotional weight of investing it all in a single moment feels genuinely difficult to act on without a structured plan.

## A note on the difference between DCA and simply investing your paycheck gradually

It's worth restating a distinction touched on earlier in this chapter, since it resolves a subtle but common point of confusion: someone who has never had a lump sum at all, and has simply been investing a portion of each paycheck as it arrives since the day they opened their account, has never actually needed a DCA schedule in the formal sense this chapter describes, because there was never a large, sitting sum to spread out in the first place. Their ongoing paycheck contributions are already, structurally, an interval-based investing pattern, arriving and getting invested steadily over time. The specific, bounded DCA schedule this chapter builds — with a defined total, interval, and endpoint — solves a different, narrower problem: what to do with an existing lump sum that's currently sitting entirely in cash, which is a meaningfully different starting situation from a steady paycheck that's never accumulated into an uninvested pile in the first place.

## A note on the emotional value of a written plan, separate from the math

It's worth closing this chapter on a point that isn't strictly mechanical but matters practically: the specific value of writing this chapter's four inputs down in advance, per the earlier short exercise, isn't only that it produces a technically correct schedule. It's that a written, specific plan is considerably harder to abandon mid-course than a vague intention was to begin with. "I'm going to invest this gradually" is a sentiment, easily reconsidered the moment the market has an uncomfortable week. "I'm investing $1,000 on the first of each month for six months, automated through my brokerage" is a specific, already-in-motion commitment, and reversing it requires an active, deliberate decision to interrupt something already running, rather than simply failing to follow through on a vague intention that was never concretely started in the first place. This difference — between a plan you have to actively break versus an intention you simply never acted on — is a large part of why the specificity this chapter insists on matters as much as the underlying math does.

# Chapter 8 — Making Your First Trade

## The situation

A chef has money in a newly opened brokerage account, has selected a fund using Chapter 5's framework and confirmed its expense ratio using Chapter 6's, and has arrived at the actual purchase screen inside her brokerage's app — and freezes. The screen presents a set of choices she doesn't recognize: an order type dropdown offering "market" and "limit," a field asking for either a dollar amount or a number of shares, and a confirmation screen with numbers she isn't certain she's reading correctly. She closes the app without completing the trade, telling herself she'll come back to it once she understands it better, a delay that has already happened twice before.

## The mechanics

A **market order** instructs your brokerage to buy (or sell) immediately, at whatever the current market price happens to be at the moment the order executes. For a widely traded, highly liquid fund — the kind of broad market index fund or ETF Chapter 5 steers a beginner toward — the price you actually pay on a market order will typically be extremely close to the price you saw on screen a moment before submitting, since these funds trade in enormous volume with a very narrow gap between what buyers are willing to pay and what sellers are willing to accept, a gap known as the bid-ask spread. For a beginner's first trade in a widely held, highly liquid fund, a market order is almost always the simplest, most appropriate choice.

A **limit order** instructs your brokerage to buy (or sell) only at a specific price you set, or better — the order will wait, potentially for hours, days, or indefinitely, until the market reaches your specified price, and may never execute at all if it doesn't. Limit orders exist to give you precise control over your execution price, which matters more for a thinly traded security with a wide bid-ask spread, or for someone with a specific price target in mind for a more speculative or volatile holding. For a first trade in a broad, liquid index fund, the added complexity of a limit order rarely buys you a meaningfully better price than a simple market order would have gotten anyway, and it introduces the real possibility of the order simply never executing if your specified price is never reached.

A distinction worth understanding clearly before your first trade: an ETF trades continuously throughout the trading day, the same way an individual stock does, with a price that moves in real time as buyers and sellers transact. A traditional mutual fund, by contrast, is priced only once per day, at its net asset value (NAV), calculated after markets close — meaning an order placed for a mutual fund during the trading day doesn't execute at the price you saw on screen at that moment; it executes at whatever the fund's NAV turns out to be once calculated after the market closes that day, which can differ, sometimes meaningfully in a volatile session, from the price displayed earlier. This is a real, mechanical difference between the two vehicle types, not a flaw in either — it's simply important to understand which one you're buying and what price you should expect the order to actually fill at.

Once a trade executes, it doesn't instantly, legally finalize — it settles, per Chapter 1's definition, generally one business day later under the current U.S. settlement rule. This mostly matters for a specific edge case: if you sell a holding and immediately try to use the full proceeds for something else, like an immediate withdrawal or another purchase requiring the exact cash amount, you may find the funds aren't fully available until settlement completes, a detail that occasionally surprises a first-time investor who assumed a completed trade meant instantly available cash.

## The framework: the first-trade checklist

**1. Confirm the ticker symbol carefully before searching.** Similarly named tickers for entirely different securities are a real and avoidable source of mistakes — double-check the exact ticker against the fund's official fact sheet or your brokerage's own research page before searching for it, rather than typing from memory.

**2. Confirm you're looking at the fund you actually intend to buy.** Once the ticker pulls up a result, confirm the fund name, provider, and expense ratio all match what you researched in Chapter 6, since a near-identical ticker occasionally belongs to a genuinely different fund than the one you intended.

**3. Choose a market order for a first trade in a broad, liquid fund.** Per this chapter's mechanics section, the added complexity of a limit order is rarely worth it for a first purchase in a widely held index fund or ETF.

**4. Enter either a dollar amount or a share count, whichever your brokerage supports.** Most modern brokerages support entering a specific dollar amount directly, using fractional-share functionality behind the scenes to fill that exact amount — this is generally the simpler, more intuitive choice for a beginner over calculating a precise share count yourself.

**5. Review the confirmation screen before submitting.** Confirm the ticker, the order type, the dollar amount or share count, and, for a mutual fund specifically, that you understand the order will fill at a NAV calculated after market close rather than at a price shown on screen right now.

**6. Submit the order, and don't expect an instant, dramatic confirmation.** A successfully placed order typically shows up simply as a filled position in your account within moments (for a market order on a liquid ETF) or by the following morning (for a mutual fund priced after that day's close) — there's no ceremony to it, and the mundaneness of the actual execution is, itself, a useful thing to know in advance, since some first-time investors expect something more dramatic and worry, incorrectly, that nothing happened.

## Worked example

The chef from this chapter's opening returns to the purchase screen with this checklist in hand. She confirms the ticker against the fund's official fact sheet, matching it exactly to avoid a similarly named but different fund she'd noticed in an earlier search. She selects a market order, enters a specific dollar amount rather than calculating a share count herself, and reviews the confirmation screen, noting the ticker and dollar amount match her intention exactly. She submits the order and, within a few minutes, sees a new position reflecting her purchase in her account — no dramatic confirmation, no unusual screen, simply a small new line item showing shares of the fund she researched, purchased at a price within a fraction of a percent of what she'd seen on screen moments before submitting. The entire process, once she understood what each screen element meant, took under two minutes.

## Common rookie mistakes to check against directly

**Confusing a similarly named or similarly ticker'd security.** Some tickers differ by a single letter and represent entirely different, unrelated securities — always confirm the fund name and provider match, not just that the ticker looks approximately right.

**Placing a large market order for a thinly traded security without checking the bid-ask spread first.** This matters far less for a broad, highly liquid index fund, but becomes a real consideration for a more niche or thinly traded holding, where a market order can execute at a price meaningfully worse than the last displayed price if there isn't much trading volume at that moment.

**Not checking a mutual fund's daily cutoff time.** Orders placed after a fund's specific daily cutoff (commonly, though not universally, around the close of regular market trading hours) typically roll over to price at the following business day's NAV instead of the current day's — worth confirming directly with your brokerage if the exact timing matters to you for a specific purchase.

**Mistaking a cash balance for an invested position.** Per Chapter 1's core warning, confirm after any deposit that the money has actually been used to purchase something, rather than assuming a funded account is automatically an invested one.

## A short exercise before your first trade

Before placing a real trade, use your brokerage's demo mode or paper-trading feature, if available, to walk through this exact checklist once with no real money involved — searching the ticker, selecting a market order, entering a dollar amount, and reviewing a confirmation screen. If no demo mode is available, walk through the same steps with real money at a small, comfortable dollar amount first, specifically to familiarize yourself with the screens and confirmations before committing a larger sum in a subsequent trade.

## A note on extended-hours trading

Some brokerages allow orders to be placed and executed outside standard market hours, commonly called pre-market or after-hours trading. Trading volume during these extended sessions is typically far lower than during standard market hours, which widens the bid-ask spread discussed earlier in this chapter and increases the odds a market order executes at a price meaningfully different from the last standard-hours price. For a first trade in a broad, liquid index fund, there's no real advantage to using an extended-hours session, and the added price uncertainty works against the exact simplicity this chapter's framework is built around — placing your first trade during standard market hours, when liquidity is at its highest, is the more sensible default until you have a specific, informed reason to do otherwise.

## A note on modifying or canceling an order before it fills

An order that hasn't yet executed can typically be canceled or modified directly through your brokerage's order-management screen, usually located wherever pending or open orders are listed. This matters most for a limit order, which, per this chapter's mechanics section, can sit unfilled for an extended period if the market never reaches your specified price — if your circumstances or intentions change while an order is still pending, canceling it is a normal, penalty-free action, not a mistake to feel embarrassed about. A market order, by contrast, typically executes within moments of submission for a liquid holding during standard trading hours, leaving little practical window to cancel it before it fills — which is one more reason a market order is the simpler, more predictable choice for a first trade, per this chapter's framework: there's no pending state to manage or worry about after submission.

## Frequently misunderstood point: a paper loss the day after your first trade isn't a mistake

A specific, common moment of alarm for a first-time investor: checking the account the day after a first purchase and seeing the balance is slightly lower than what was invested. This is an entirely ordinary, expected feature of a security whose price moves continuously, not a sign the trade was placed incorrectly or that a mistake was made. A broad market index fund's price moves up and down on essentially every trading day, for reasons that have nothing to do with the mechanics of how or when you bought it — a single day's decline, even the day immediately following a first purchase, carries no more significance than any other single day's ordinary movement would. Reacting to a routine, single-day paper loss by selling, second-guessing the fund choice, or abandoning the plan entirely is a far more costly mistake than the paper loss itself, which reflects nothing more than the ordinary, expected volatility of owning anything that trades in a public market.

## A note on stop orders and other order types you likely don't need yet

Beyond the market and limit orders covered in this chapter's core mechanics, most brokerages offer additional order types — a stop order, which becomes a market order once a security reaches a specified trigger price, commonly used to attempt to limit a loss on an existing position, and variations combining stop and limit features together. These exist for more active trading strategies and carry their own mechanical nuances and risks — a stop order, in a fast-moving, volatile market, can execute at a price considerably worse than its trigger price, a detail that surprises traders who assume a stop order guarantees a specific exit price, which it doesn't. For the specific goal this book is built around — a first purchase of a broad, diversified, long-horizon core holding — none of these additional order types are necessary, and introducing them prematurely adds complexity without a corresponding benefit for a first-time investor's actual situation. They're worth knowing exist, and worth returning to only if a specific, informed reason to use one arises later.

## Common objections and how to handle them

**"What if I place an order and immediately realize I made a mistake?"** If the order hasn't filled yet, per the cancellation note earlier in this chapter, cancel it directly through your brokerage's order-management screen. If it has already filled, you generally can't "undo" a filled trade, but you can typically place an offsetting trade — selling what you just bought, if the mistake was significant enough to warrant it — understanding that a very recent buy-then-sell pair may realize a small loss from the bid-ask spread alone, a minor, bounded cost worth accepting over compounding the original mistake by leaving it in place out of reluctance to reverse it.

**"How do I know my order actually executed at a fair price?"** For a widely traded ETF or index fund during standard market hours, the executed price will typically sit extremely close to the price displayed just before you submitted the order, per this chapter's discussion of tight bid-ask spreads on liquid securities. Your brokerage's trade confirmation, generated immediately after execution, shows the exact price and time your order filled — comparing that against the price you saw on screen moments earlier is a reasonable, quick sanity check for a first trade, though a small difference of a few cents per share is normal and not a sign anything went wrong.

## A note on what your account statement shows after a first trade

After a first trade settles, your brokerage account will typically display a position showing the ticker, the number of shares (or fractional shares) held, the current market value, and, often, your original cost basis — the price you originally paid, used later for tax purposes when the holding is eventually sold in a taxable account. It's worth taking a moment, the first time this appears, to locate each of these fields and confirm you understand what each one represents, since this same layout is what every future check-in, rebalancing review, and annual review throughout the rest of this book will involve reading. A first trade isn't just a transaction — it's also the first time the ongoing account-reading skill this book's later chapters assume gets put into practice for real.

## A note on the specific, ordinary anticlimax of a first trade

It's worth stating plainly, as a closing note to this chapter, that a first trade is very often a genuine anticlimax, and that this is a feature, not a disappointment. After months, sometimes years, of hesitation and vocabulary-clearing, the actual moment of placing a first trade typically takes under two minutes and produces no dramatic feedback of any kind — no congratulatory message, no visible transformation, just a small new line item in an account that looked, seconds earlier, exactly the same as it always had. Some first-time investors expect the moment to feel more significant than it does, and are mildly deflated when it doesn't. The significance was never going to be in the moment of the click — it's in the fact that a mechanical obstacle that had been standing in the way for months or years is now, quietly and permanently, resolved, and every future contribution from this point forward inherits the benefit of that resolution without needing to feel dramatic to be real.

## A worked example: placing a recurring order versus a one-time order

To close this chapter with a concrete distinction worth understanding clearly: a one-time order, of the kind this chapter's checklist has walked through, is a single, discrete transaction executed once. A recurring order, the mechanism underlying Chapter 7's dollar-cost-averaging schedule and this book's broader emphasis on automation, is a standing instruction that repeats on a defined schedule without requiring you to revisit the purchase screen each time. Setting one up typically involves the same ticker-confirmation and dollar-amount steps as a one-time order, plus an additional step selecting the recurrence frequency (weekly, biweekly, or monthly, most commonly) and the funding source it should draw from automatically. A first-time investor executing their very first purchase manually, per this chapter's checklist, and then immediately setting up a recurring order for all subsequent contributions, has effectively used this chapter's mechanics exactly once by hand and then handed the repeated version of the same task to automation — the correct sequence for nearly every reader of this book, since the manual first trade builds the muscle memory this chapter is meant to provide, while the recurring order that follows it removes the need to keep exercising that muscle every single month going forward.

# Chapter 9 — Rebalancing

## Triggers, not guesses

### The situation

A logistics coordinator set up an 80/20 stock-to-bond allocation across two funds two years ago, funded it consistently, and hasn't looked at the actual balance between the two since. A strong run for stocks relative to bonds over that period has quietly shifted the real allocation to something closer to 88/12, though he has no idea this has happened, since nothing about his account has prompted him to check, and the shift happened gradually enough that no single month's statement made it obvious.

### The mechanics

Rebalancing is the practice of periodically bringing a portfolio's actual allocation back in line with its intended target, correcting for the drift that naturally occurs as different holdings grow at different rates over time. The mechanism behind the drift is simple: if stocks outperform bonds over a given period, the stock portion of a portfolio grows to represent a larger share of the total than originally intended, purely as a function of relative performance, with no deliberate action required on your part to cause it. Left unaddressed indefinitely, this drift can meaningfully increase a portfolio's actual risk level beyond what was originally chosen — an 80/20 allocation that's quietly become 88/12 is carrying more concentrated stock-market risk than the investor originally decided was appropriate for their situation, even though no explicit decision to increase that risk was ever made.

Two common, well-established approaches exist for deciding when to rebalance, both referenced directly in Vanguard's own published research on the subject, and either is a reasonable, legitimate choice.

**Calendar-based rebalancing** checks and corrects the allocation on a fixed schedule — commonly annually, sometimes semi-annually — regardless of how much drift has actually occurred by that date. Its appeal is simplicity: a single, recurring calendar reminder, checked once a year, with no ongoing monitoring required between checks.

**Threshold-based rebalancing** checks the allocation periodically but only actually rebalances once a holding has drifted beyond a predetermined number of percentage points from its target — a common threshold is five percentage points, though the specific number is a matter of preference rather than a fixed rule. Its appeal is precision: rebalancing happens only when drift has become meaningful, rather than on a fixed calendar regardless of whether any real correction is actually needed at that point.

Mechanically, rebalancing itself is straightforward once triggered: sell a portion of the overweighted holding and use the proceeds to buy more of the underweighted one, restoring the target percentages. Inside a tax-advantaged account — an IRA or 401(k) — this transaction has no tax consequence at all, since gains and losses inside these accounts aren't taxed as they occur. Inside a taxable brokerage account, selling an appreciated holding to rebalance can trigger a taxable capital gain, which is worth factoring into the decision. A commonly used technique to reduce or avoid this cost in a taxable account is to rebalance using new contributions first — directing new money specifically toward the underweighted holding rather than immediately selling the overweighted one — and only selling the overweighted holding outright if new contributions alone aren't sufficient to fully close the gap.

## The framework: choosing and executing a trigger

**Step 1 — Choose calendar-based or threshold-based rebalancing, explicitly, in advance.** Either is legitimate; the value is in committing to one method deliberately rather than rebalancing reactively based on how the market happens to feel in a given week, which tends to produce poorly timed, emotionally driven decisions rather than a disciplined, rules-based correction.

**Step 2 — Set a concrete mechanism to actually check.** For calendar-based rebalancing, this means a recurring calendar reminder on a specific date each year. For threshold-based rebalancing, this means a periodic check-in — quarterly is a common cadence — specifically to measure current drift against your chosen threshold, even if no action is taken at most of those check-ins.

**Step 3 — When triggered, rebalance using new contributions first, in a taxable account.** Direct upcoming contributions specifically toward the underweighted holding until the gap closes, before considering an outright sale of the overweighted position, to minimize or avoid triggering a taxable capital gain.

**Step 4 — If new contributions alone aren't sufficient to close the gap, sell the overweighted holding and buy the underweighted one directly.** In a tax-advantaged account, this is straightforward and carries no tax consequence. In a taxable account, factor the resulting capital gain into your decision, and consider consulting a tax professional if the gain is substantial.

**Step 5 — Reset your baseline after rebalancing and repeat the process at the next scheduled check.** Rebalancing isn't a one-time correction — it's a recurring maintenance habit, matching the ongoing nature of market movement itself.

## Worked example

The logistics coordinator from this chapter's opening discovers, during a review prompted by this chapter, that his

80/20 target has drifted to 88/12. He adopts a threshold-based approach going forward, choosing a five-percentage-point threshold, and confirms this drift exceeds it, triggering a correction now. Since most of his holdings sit inside a 401(k) and an IRA — both tax-advantaged — he simply sells enough of the overweighted stock fund and buys the underweighted bond fund to restore the 80/20 target directly, with no tax consequence to consider. He sets a recurring quarterly calendar reminder going forward, specifically to check drift against his five-point threshold, rather than letting another two years pass unmonitored.

## A second worked example: rebalancing in a taxable account

An investor with a similar allocation drift, but held entirely inside a taxable brokerage account, applies Step 3 first rather than immediately selling: for the next several months, new contributions are directed entirely toward the underweighted bond fund rather than split proportionally across both holdings, gradually closing the gap without triggering any sale of the appreciated stock position. After four months, the gap has closed enough to fall back under the five-point threshold using new contributions alone, avoiding a taxable event entirely — a meaningfully different, and often preferable, path to the same destination compared to an outright sale, available specifically because the drift wasn't so large that new contributions alone were insufficient to close it within a reasonable window.

## Common objections and how to handle them

**"Isn't rebalancing just selling my winners to buy my losers — doesn't that work against me?"** This is a common, understandable intuition, but it inverts the actual purpose. Rebalancing isn't a bet that the underweighted holding will outperform going forward — it's a discipline for maintaining a consistent, deliberately chosen risk level over time, regardless of which holding happens to be performing better in a given period. The goal is risk management, not performance prediction.

**"How often should I actually check, even under a calendar-based approach?"** Once a year is a common, well-supported default under a calendar-based approach —

frequent enough to prevent significant drift from accumulating unchecked, infrequent enough to avoid over-managing a long-horizon portfolio based on short-term market noise.

**"What if I have a target-date fund or an all-in-one fund that already rebalances internally?"** Many target-date and all-in-one balanced funds handle rebalancing automatically as part of their internal fund management, adjusting their own underlying holdings without requiring any action from you. If your entire portfolio consists of a single fund like this, this chapter's manual framework doesn't apply to you directly — confirm with the fund's own documentation that automatic internal rebalancing is genuinely part of its structure before assuming it, since not every multi-asset fund handles this identically.

## A short exercise before your next check-in

Write down your intended target allocation explicitly — the specific percentage split across your major holding categories — if you haven't already done so in writing. Then check your account's actual current allocation against that target. If you've never done this before, treat this as your Step 1 check-in regardless of which trigger method you eventually settle on going forward, and use the result to decide whether this chapter's Step 3 and Step 4 apply to your situation right now.

## A note on rebalancing across multiple accounts as a single portfolio

Someone holding a 401(k), an IRA, and a taxable brokerage account simultaneously has, in effect, one overall portfolio spread across three separate account statements, not three unrelated portfolios that each need their own independent target allocation. The more precise version of this chapter's framework treats your target allocation as applying to the total across every account combined, and checks drift against that combined total, rather than checking each account in isolation against the same target individually. This matters because it opens up a meaningfully better version of Step 3's taxable-account tax-efficiency technique: rather than rebalancing inside a taxable account by selling an appreciated holding and triggering a capital gain, it's often possible to correct the same overall drift entirely inside a tax-advantaged account instead, where a sale carries no tax consequence at all — shifting the correction to whichever account makes it cheapest, rather than defaulting to correcting drift separately, and identically, inside every account it happens to show up in. Building this combined view requires a bit more manual tracking, generally a simple spreadsheet listing every holding across every account with its current value, but for an investor with meaningful taxable-account holdings, the tax savings from rebalancing preferentially inside tax-advantaged accounts can be a genuinely worthwhile trade for that extra bit of manual bookkeeping.

## Frequently misunderstood point: rebalancing isn't a reaction to news

A specific, avoidable mistake to guard against directly: treating a significant news event — an earnings report, a rate announcement, a geopolitical development — as a cue to check and adjust your allocation outside your predetermined schedule. This isn't what either trigger method in this chapter describes, and reacting to news on an ad hoc basis reintroduces exactly the emotionally driven, poorly timed decision-making that a disciplined, rules-based trigger is built to prevent in the first place. If a specific news event genuinely causes meaningful drift beyond your chosen threshold, a threshold-based approach will already flag it at your next scheduled check-in without requiring you to react to the news itself — the trigger is drift, not headlines, and conflating the two undoes the entire discipline this chapter is teaching.

## A note on rebalancing when your target allocation itself has changed

Everything in this chapter so far has assumed a fixed target allocation that the actual portfolio drifts away from and gets corrected back toward. But the target itself is allowed to change, deliberately, as your own circumstances change — a goal moving closer in time, a shift in genuine risk tolerance, a major life change. When the target changes, the correction isn't really "rebalancing" in the sense this chapter has used the term so far — drifting back to an old target — it's a deliberate reallocation to a new one, and it's worth treating as its own distinct decision, made consciously and, ideally, not too frequently, rather than something adjusted casually every time the market has a rough week and tests your stated risk tolerance. A target allocation revisited once a year, alongside the annual review this chapter's framework already calls for, and left alone otherwise, tends to produce better outcomes than one that's second-guessed and revised reactively throughout the year.

## Common objections and how to handle them

**"Doesn't frequent rebalancing cost more in trading costs or taxes than it saves in risk control?"** For most retail investors using commission-free trades inside primarily tax-advantaged accounts, the direct trading cost of rebalancing is close to zero, and the tax cost, per this chapter's guidance, can be minimized or avoided using the new-contributions technique and by preferring tax-advantaged accounts for any outright sale. Rebalancing too frequently — reacting to every small, ordinary daily fluctuation rather than a genuine threshold breach — is a real inefficiency, but a properly triggered annual or threshold-based rebalance, following this chapter's framework, isn't the version of "too frequent" this objection is actually worried about.

**"What if I genuinely don't know what my target allocation should be in the first place?"** This chapter assumes a target has already been chosen, using Chapter 5's core-and-explore framework for the equity-versus-individual-stock split and, more broadly, an informed judgment about your own risk tolerance and time horizon for the stock-versus-bond split noted in Chapter 5. If you're genuinely uncertain where to start, a fee-only financial advisor can help translate your specific goals and risk tolerance into a concrete starting target, which this chapter's rebalancing framework can then maintain going forward.

## A note on rebalancing as your goal's timeline shortens

A specific, deliberate exception to the "don't react to short-term events" discipline described earlier in this chapter: as a specific, dated goal draws meaningfully closer — a few years out rather than decades — a planned, gradual shift toward a more conservative target allocation (a higher bond percentage, a lower stock percentage) is a normal, appropriate part of an evolving plan, distinct from a reactive rebalance triggered by market news. This is a deliberate change to the target itself, per the earlier note on target changes, timed to the calendar of your own goal rather than to market conditions, and it's worth planning this glide path in advance, as your goal's date comes into clearer view, rather than treating your target allocation as permanently fixed from the day you first set it.

## A worked example: a full annual rebalancing cycle over three years

To show this chapter's framework operating across more than a single correction, consider an investor who sets an 80/20 target and adopts calendar-based rebalancing, checking every year on the same date. Year one's check finds the allocation has drifted to 83/17 after a strong year for stocks — within a reasonable range for many threshold-based investors, but under a strict calendar-based approach, the investor corrects it back to 80/20 regardless, selling a portion of the stock fund and buying the bond fund inside a tax-advantaged account with no tax consequence. Year two's check, after a weaker year for stocks and a stronger one for bonds, finds the allocation has drifted the other direction, to 76/24, and the investor again corrects back to 80/20, this time selling a portion of the bond fund and buying the stock fund — a reminder that rebalancing works in both directions, not only trimming an overperforming stock allocation. Year three's check finds only a 1-percentage-point drift, well within any reasonable threshold, and the investor, still following the calendar-based approach consistently, makes a token correction back to the exact target regardless, maintaining the discipline of the fixed schedule even when the dollar amount involved is small. Across all three years, no single correction was large, no correction was triggered by news or emotion, and the portfolio's actual risk level never drifted meaningfully far from what the investor originally decided was appropriate — the entire, unglamorous point of this chapter's framework, demonstrated across a realistic multi-year stretch rather than a single isolated correction.

## A note on rebalancing a portfolio that includes an explore allocation

For a reader who adopted Chapter 5's core-and-explore structure, rebalancing applies a little differently to each piece. The core holding — the broad index fund or funds — follows this chapter's framework directly, checked against a defined stock-to-bond target using either trigger method. The explore allocation, by its nature, is expected to drift more than the core, sometimes considerably, since individual holdings carry more volatility than a diversified fund by design; the relevant question for the explore allocation isn't whether it has drifted from an internal target among the individual positions within it, but whether the entire explore allocation, as a share of the total portfolio, has grown beyond the ceiling you set for it back in Chapter 5's self-assessment exercise. If a strong run in a single explore holding has pushed the explore allocation from an intended 10% up to 18% of the total portfolio, that's a meaningful signal worth acting on using this chapter's same trigger logic — trimming the explore allocation back toward its intended ceiling, not because the individual holding did anything wrong, but because the overall portfolio's risk concentration has grown beyond what was originally decided.

## A short exercise: setting your own rebalancing calendar right now

Before closing this chapter, open your phone's calendar app and set a single recurring annual reminder, dated to whenever you're reading this, labeled plainly — "check investment allocation" is sufficient. This is the entire mechanical requirement for calendar-based rebalancing, and doing it now, while the chapter is fresh, is meaningfully more likely to actually happen than deciding to "get around to it eventually." If you've chosen threshold-based rebalancing instead, set the same reminder at a shorter interval — quarterly is a reasonable default — labeled as a check-in rather than a guaranteed action, since a threshold-based check may find nothing to correct most quarters and that's the expected, healthy outcome of the method, not a wasted reminder.

# Chapter 10 — The First-Year Action Checklist

## The situation

The nurse from Chapter 1, having worked through every chapter of this book in order, wants one final, consolidated version of everything she's learned — not another concept to absorb, but a concrete, month-by-month plan she can follow for the next twelve months without having to reconstruct the sequence from nine separate chapters each time she needs to remember what comes next.

## The mechanics

Every mechanical piece covered across this book has a natural place in a first-year timeline, and laying them out in sequence turns nine chapters of individual mechanics into a single, followable plan. This chapter doesn't introduce new mechanics — it's a synthesis, built specifically to be reread and followed literally during your actual first year, the way the rest of this book's chapters are built to be reread individually as their specific topic becomes relevant.

## The framework: month by month

**Month 1 — Vocabulary and account selection.** Work through Chapter 1's five-point vocabulary framework until you can define each term without looking it up. Apply Chapter 2's six-point brokerage scorecard to two or three candidate brokerages and select one.

**Month 1, continued — Account type and opening.** Apply Chapter 3's framework to determine which account type (or types) to open first, given your employment situation, and complete the actual account-opening process at your selected brokerage. If an employer 401(k) is available and you haven't enrolled, confirm your enrollment status and contribution percentage with HR this same month.

**Month 2 — Funding order and first deposit.** Run your available monthly investing amount through Chapter 4's funding waterfall, confirming your employer match is captured, your starter buffer exists, any high-interest debt is factored in, and the remainder is sequenced across tax-advantaged and taxable accounts correctly. Make your first deposit into your newly opened account.

**Month 2, continued — Fund selection.** Apply Chapter 5's core-and-explore framework to decide on your core holding, and use Chapter 6's expense-ratio framework to confirm you've selected a low-cost option among your candidates.

**Month 3 — First trade, or the start of a DCA schedule.** If you're investing a lump sum, apply Chapter 7's framework to build and automate a dollar-cost-averaging schedule. If you're investing your first regular contribution with no lump sum involved, apply Chapter 8's first-trade checklist directly and execute your first purchase this month.

**Months 3 through 8 (or the length of your chosen DCA schedule) — Steady execution.** Let your automated recurring purchases or DCA schedule run without interruption. Resist the urge to check your balance daily or to make reactive changes based on short-term market movement — per Chapter 7's honest treatment of the research, the value of a disciplined schedule comes specifically from not second-guessing it mid-course.

**Month 6 — First allocation check-in.** Whether or not any rebalancing is needed yet, use Chapter 9's framework to write down your intended target allocation explicitly for the first time, if you haven't already, and check your actual allocation against it. At six months in, meaningful drift is unlikely, but establishing the habit of checking is the point of this early check-in, not correcting drift that likely hasn't yet occurred.

**Month 9 — Funding waterfall review.** Rerun Chapter 4's waterfall against any changes since Month 2 — a raise, a paid-off debt, a fully funded buffer — and adjust your contribution allocation accordingly if any input has changed.

**Month 12 — Full annual review.** Apply Chapter 9's rebalancing framework in full, checking your actual allocation against your target and rebalancing if your chosen trigger (calendar or threshold) indicates it's warranted. Confirm your annual contribution totals against current IRA and 401(k) contribution limits, and note that any taxable brokerage account activity — dividends received, or any shares sold during the year — will generate tax documents (commonly a 1099 form) arriving from your brokerage early in the following year, a mechanical heads-up worth knowing about in advance rather than being surprised by come tax season; this is a note about document arrival, not tax advice, and any actual tax questions belong with a qualified tax professional.

**Year two and beyond.** Repeat the annual rhythm established in Months 6 through 12: a mid-year allocation check-in, a funding waterfall review whenever a major input changes, and a full annual review each year matching Month 12's process. The mechanics don't change year over year — only the specific numbers do, as your income, goals, and account balances evolve.

## Worked example

The nurse from Chapter 1 follows this exact timeline. By the end of Month 1, she's selected a brokerage using the six-point scorecard and opened a Roth IRA, having confirmed her income falls under the eligibility threshold and that she has no employer 401(k) available at her current job. By Month 2, she's run her $8,000 plus an ongoing $350 a month through the funding waterfall, confirming she has no high-interest debt and an adequate starter buffer already in place, and selects a broad market index fund as her core holding after confirming its expense ratio compares favorably against alternatives. By Month 3, she builds a six-month DCA schedule for her $8,000 lump sum and sets her ongoing $350 monthly contribution to begin immediately alongside it, both automated through her brokerage's recurring purchase feature. She checks her allocation at Month 6 for the first time, finds no meaningful drift yet, as expected, and confirms the habit is in place. At Month 12, she runs a full review, finds her allocation still within her chosen five-point threshold and no rebalancing needed yet, and confirms her total contributions for the year against the current IRA limit, noting she has some remaining room to potentially increase her monthly contribution the following year. What took ten chapters and roughly two years of prior hesitation to fully understand has become, in practice, a single followable year, and an ongoing annual rhythm from that point forward.

## A second worked example: a reader with an employer plan already running

A separate reader begins this same timeline from a different starting point — he already has a 401(k) through his employer, auto-enrolled at a modest default contribution percentage when he was hired two years ago, but has never opened anything else and has never actually looked at what his 401(k) is invested in. His Month 1 looks different from the nurse's: instead of opening a brand-new account, he confirms his current 401(k) contribution percentage against Chapter 4's Step 1 and finds he's already capturing the full employer match, a pleasant discovery he hadn't previously confirmed. He then applies Chapter 6's expense-ratio framework directly to the default fund he was auto-enrolled into and finds it's a reasonably priced target-date fund, requiring no change. His Month 1 also includes opening a Roth IRA at a brokerage selected through Chapter 2's scorecard, since he has an additional $250 a month he wants to invest beyond his 401(k) contribution and prefers the broader fund selection an IRA offers over his employer plan's limited menu.

By Month 2, his funding waterfall confirms the $250 belongs in the newly opened Roth IRA, per Step 4, since his match is already captured and he carries no high-interest debt. He selects a core holding using Chapter 5's framework and checks its expense ratio using Chapter 6's, exactly as the nurse did. His remaining months follow the same rhythm as the checklist above, with one difference worth noting: his Month 12 annual review now covers two accounts rather than one, and his combined allocation check, per Chapter 9's note on rebalancing across multiple accounts as a single portfolio, looks at his 401(k) and his new Roth IRA together rather than as two separate, unrelated portfolios. This is, mechanically, the same checklist as the nurse's, applied to a starting position that already had one account moving before this book's chapters were ever opened — proof that this chapter's month-by-month framework adapts to wherever a reader is actually starting from, rather than assuming everyone begins from an identical, completely blank slate.

## A closing checklist, condensed to a single page

For quick reference, independent of the month-by-month detail above: open the right account (Chapters 1 through 3). Fund it in the right order (Chapter 4). Pick a sensible core holding at a low cost (Chapters 5 and 6). Get the money invested, either through a DCA schedule or ongoing contributions (Chapter 7). Execute the actual trade correctly (Chapter 8). Check your allocation on a schedule, not a whim, and correct it only when a real trigger fires (Chapter 9). Repeat the whole rhythm annually. That's the entire mechanical content of this book, compressed into seven steps, meant to be reread the week before you take any one of them for real.

## A note for a reader starting later in the calendar year

Someone working through this book in, say, October rather than January doesn't need to wait for a new calendar year to begin this chapter's timeline — the month-by-month framework above is meant to be read as month one of your own personal timeline, starting whenever you actually begin, not as a fixed mapping to the calendar months named in the checklist. The one adjustment worth making explicitly: if you're starting late in a calendar year and have tax-advantaged contribution room you haven't yet used for that year, confirm the specific contribution deadline for your account type — some, like an IRA, generally allow contributions for a given tax year up until the tax filing deadline the following spring, while others, like a 401(k), are typically bound to contributions made within the calendar year itself through payroll. Knowing which of your account types has a hard calendar-year cutoff and which has more flexibility affects how you sequence Months 1 and 2 of your own personal timeline if you're beginning partway through a year.

## What "done" looks like at the end of your first year

It's worth being explicit about what successfully completing this chapter's timeline actually looks like in practice, since "done" here isn't a finished, closed state the way finishing a single negotiation or paying off a single debt is — it's the establishment of an ongoing, repeatable rhythm. At the end of a genuinely successful first year: you have at least one open, funded investment account, correctly matched to your situation using Chapter 3's framework. You've captured any available employer match in full. You hold a core position in a low-cost, broadly diversified fund, selected deliberately using Chapters 5 and 6 rather than by default or by guesswork. Your contributions have been automated, whether through a completed DCA schedule, ongoing recurring purchases, or both.

You've checked your allocation at least once against an explicit, written target. And you have a specific, dated plan for repeating the annual rhythm again next year. None of this requires a large account balance to count as success — the mechanical system, functioning correctly and repeatably, is the actual achievement this book has been building toward, independent of how much money happens to be running through it in year one.

## Before You Close This Book

Ten chapters, one underlying argument running through all of them: the gap between wanting to invest and actually investing was never a gap in intelligence, effort, or character. It was a gap in vocabulary and mechanics — a set of terms and steps that every other guide assumed you already had, and that this book set out to actually teach, in the order you'd need them, rather than assume them and move on to the next topic.

It's worth being honest about what this book didn't try to do. It didn't tell you which specific stock, fund, or brokerage will perform best — nobody can promise that, and any book that claimed otherwise would be selling you something other than the truth. It didn't diagnose why investing felt intimidating in the first place, or explore the psychology of financial avoidance — that's real, valuable territory, and other work covers it well. This book stayed entirely in the mechanics: what a brokerage account actually is, how to choose one, what each account type actually does, what order to fund things in, how to choose between an index fund and an individual stock, why an expense ratio matters more than its small size suggests, how to actually spread out a lump sum, how to place an actual trade, and when to correct an allocation that's drifted.

What changes once you've worked through this book isn't your risk tolerance, your income, or your certainty about what the market will do next year — none of that was ever this book's job to change. What changes is that the specific, mechanical obstacle that was standing between you and an open, funded, correctly structured investment account is gone, replaced by an actual account, actually holding something, actually growing or shrinking with the market the way every other investor's account does. That's a genuinely different starting position than the one you were in before opening this book, even though the market itself doesn't know or care that you've read it.

There's a broader habit worth carrying past this book's specific chapters. Nearly every domain that feels intimidating from the outside turns out, on closer inspection, to be a manageable set of vocabulary and mechanics that somebody simply forgot to explain to you before assuming you already knew it. Investing was this book's specific example. It won't be the last domain where that pattern shows up in your life, and the habit of assuming a gap is mechanical rather than a permanent verdict on your own competence is worth carrying into whatever the next one turns out to be.

It's also important to state plainly what this book cannot promise, because an honest accounting of that matters more than a reassuring one. Nothing in these ten chapters changes what the market actually does in any given year, decade, or moment you happen to check your balance. A correctly opened account, correctly funded in the right order, holding a correctly chosen low-cost fund, can still decline in value over a given stretch of time — that's not a flaw in this book's method, it's the ordinary nature of an asset that trades on a public market, and no mechanical framework, however sound, changes that basic fact. What this book's method changes is something narrower and, in its own way, more durable: whether you're positioned to participate in what markets have, historically, over long periods, generally rewarded patient, diversified, low-cost participation with — not a guarantee, but a real, well-documented historical pattern, distinct from a promise about any specific year or any specific dollar.

It's worth closing, too, on the specific moment this book was built around: the moment you stop reading advice about investing and actually become an investor, in the plain, mechanical sense of having money in an account, invested in something, growing or shrinking the way every other investor's money does. That moment doesn't require confidence, certainty, or a fully resolved feeling about risk. It requires the account to be open, the vocabulary to be clear enough to act on, and the first trade to be placed. Everything else — refining your allocation, learning more about individual securities if that interests you, adjusting your funding order as your income changes — is genuinely optional, ongoing refinement that happens after that first moment, not a set of prerequisites that has to be satisfied before it.

Open the account. Fund it in the right order. Pick something sensible and low-cost. Get the money in. Check on it on a schedule, not a whim. That's the whole book, and it was never more complicated than that — it just needed to be said plainly, in order, to someone who'd never been told any of it before.

# Notes & Further Reading

This book draws on established, verifiable research in index investing, fund pricing, and investor behavior throughout. Readers interested in going deeper are pointed to the original sources rather than secondary summaries.

**On the origin and case for index investing:** John Bogle, founder of Vanguard, created the first index mutual fund available to individual investors in 1976 and laid out the underlying case for low-cost, broad-market index investing at length in his own published writing, including *Common Sense on Mutual Funds: New Imperatives for the Intelligent Investor* (1999) and *The Little Book of Common Sense Investing* (2007). Burton Malkiel's long-running *A Random Walk Down Wall Street* (first published 1973, regularly updated in subsequent editions) independently develops a related case for broad diversification and skepticism of consistent stock-picking outperformance, referenced in Chapter 5.

**On active-versus-passive fund performance:** S&P; Dow Jones Indices publishes the ongoing SPIVA (S&P; Indices

Versus Active) Scorecard, a regularly updated, publicly available research report comparing actively managed fund performance against relevant benchmark indices across multiple time horizons, referenced in Chapter 5's discussion of why a broad index fund is a reasonable default for a beginner. Readers wanting current figures should consult the latest published scorecard directly, since the specific outperformance percentages are updated with each release rather than fixed.

**On dollar-cost averaging versus lump-sum investing:** Vanguard's 2012 research paper, commonly cited under the title "Dollar-cost averaging just means taking risk later," directly compares historical outcomes of dollar-cost-averaged versus lump-sum investing across multiple markets and multi-decade periods, referenced in full and honestly in Chapter 7, including its finding that lump-sum investing outperformed a DCA schedule in a majority of historical periods studied, alongside its acknowledgment of DCA's genuine behavioral and regret-reduction value.

**On brokerage account protection:** The Securities Investor Protection Corporation (SIPC), a congressionally chartered nonprofit, publishes official, publicly available information on the scope and limits of brokerage account protection in the event of a member firm's failure, referenced in Chapter 1; readers should consult SIPC's own published materials directly for current coverage limits, which are distinct from, and should not be confused with, FDIC deposit insurance covering traditional bank accounts.

**On settlement cycle rules:** The U.S. Securities and Exchange Commission's rule shortening the standard settlement cycle for most securities transactions from two business days to one business day (commonly referred to as the move from T+2 to T+1) took effect in May 2024; readers should consult the SEC's own published rule and guidance directly for the current, authoritative settlement timeline and any exceptions that may apply to specific security types.

**On investor behavior and individual trading outcomes:** Brad Barber and Terrance Odean's research on individual investor trading behavior, including their widely cited paper "Trading Is Hazardous to Your Wealth" (published in *The Journal of Finance*, 2000), examines the relationship between trading frequency and net investor returns using large brokerage account datasets, relevant background to this book's broader emphasis on a disciplined, low-turnover approach over frequent, reactive trading.

**On rebalancing methodology:** Vanguard has published research directly addressing calendar-based versus threshold-based rebalancing approaches and their relative tradeoffs, referenced generally in Chapter 9; readers wanting a deeper treatment of the specific historical performance differences between rebalancing methods should consult Vanguard's own published research library directly.

**On retirement account rules and contribution limits:** The U.S. Internal Revenue Service publishes official, regularly updated guidance on IRA and 401(k) contribution limits, income-based Roth IRA eligibility phase-outs, early-withdrawal penalty rules and their exceptions, and required minimum distribution rules, referenced generally throughout Chapters 3 and 4; specific dollar limits and thresholds are adjusted periodically and should always be verified directly through current IRS guidance or a plan administrator rather than any figure that might otherwise be quoted here and go stale.

**On compound growth mathematics:** The compounding calculations referenced in Chapter 6 follow standard, widely available future-value formulas taught in any introductory finance curriculum; readers wanting to run their own precise numbers are pointed to reputable, free compound-interest and fee-impact calculators published by major financial regulators and institutions, including the U.S. Securities and Exchange Commission's own investor-education tools, rather than a single proprietary source.

**On investor-education resources for account mechanics generally:** The U.S. Securities and Exchange Commission maintains Investor.gov, a free, official investor-education resource covering brokerage account basics, order types, fee structures, and how to verify a firm's registration status, referenced generally throughout Chapters 1, 2, and 8. The Financial Industry Regulatory Authority (FINRA) similarly maintains free investor-education materials and the BrokerCheck tool for verifying a brokerage or investment professional's registration and disciplinary history, referenced in

Chapter 2's discussion of confirming a brokerage is a genuine, regulated firm.

**On industry-wide fund fee trends:** The Investment Company Institute (ICI), a national association representing the U.S. registered fund industry, publishes an annual report on trends in mutual fund and ETF expense ratios across the industry, providing a useful, independently tracked longitudinal reference for the general decline in fund costs referenced in Chapter 6; readers wanting current, precise industry-average figures should consult ICI's most recently published edition directly rather than any figure that might otherwise be referenced here and age quickly.

A methodological note on how sources were used in writing this book: every named researcher, institution, book, or study cited above was verified against its actual, publicly documented existence and general findings before being included here. No statistic, percentage, or specific study finding appears anywhere in this book's chapters without a traceable source in this section. Passages describing general mechanics without a specific citation attached — the five-point vocabulary framework in

Chapter 1, the six-point brokerage scorecard in Chapter 2, the funding waterfall in Chapter 4, the month-by-month checklist in Chapter 10 — reflect the author's own applied framework, built from standard financial mechanics and practitioner experience, and are presented explicitly as that, not disguised as independently published research findings.

A note on the dollar figures, expense ratios, contribution limits, and assumed rates of return used throughout the worked examples in every chapter: they are illustrative only, chosen to make each mechanism concrete and easy to follow, not to represent verified current fee schedules, guaranteed returns, or advice to apply directly to your own accounts. Actual investment returns vary meaningfully year to year and are never guaranteed at any specific figure, including the 7% planning assumption used in Chapter 6. Fund expense ratios, brokerage features, and IRS contribution limits all change over time and should always be verified directly against current, official sources before being relied on. Readers should always substitute their own researched numbers and, for anything involving tax treatment, account eligibility, or investment selection, consult a qualified, licensed professional rather than treating any example in this book as personalized advice.

This book is not legal, tax, investment, or financial advice, and nothing in it should be treated as a guarantee of any specific investment outcome. Tax treatment of investment accounts, contribution limits, brokerage fee structures, and withdrawal rules vary by jurisdiction, account type, and change over time; readers are strongly encouraged to consult a qualified financial advisor, accountant, or tax professional before making significant decisions based on the frameworks in this book.

# About

The Investment Onboarding Playbook is part of the Wealth Mechanics library — a series covering the concrete, learnable mechanics behind everyday money decisions: negotiation, debt payoff, pricing, automated saving systems, savings rate, and, in this volume, the specific mechanical steps behind actually opening and funding a first investment account. Where some books explore the psychology behind why money decisions feel hard, Wealth Mechanics stays entirely in the mechanics: what to actually do, in what order, and why each step is built the way it is.

Every book in this library follows the same shape — a real situation, the mechanics underneath it, a concrete framework you can apply immediately, and a worked example showing it applied start to finish with real, illustrative numbers. None of them ask you to become a different kind of investor, saver, or negotiator before you can use them. They're built to be reopened whenever the specific mechanic they cover becomes relevant again — a first paycheck, a first employer match, a first lump sum, a first year of an allocation that's quietly drifted.

Daniel Cross writes the Wealth Mechanics library from the practitioner's side of the account-opening screen — years spent walking people through the exact moment where financial advice stops being abstract and starts requiring an actual click, an actual ticker symbol, an actual dollar amount entered into an actual field, and watching how often a genuinely capable, motivated person got stuck at that moment for want of someone willing to explain the vocabulary plainly. The pen name reflects the series' identity rather than a single individual's biography: a direct, mechanics-first voice focused entirely on usable steps, distinct in both subject and style from the psychological, pattern-diagnosis approach of this studio's sibling series, The Money Instinct, which explores the wired-in reflexes behind money behavior rather than the specific mechanics behind a given financial decision.

This volume connects closely to two others in the library, and it's worth being clear about how the three divide the territory. *The Automatic Wealth System* covers how to build a bank-account structure and automate transfers so saving happens without relying on willpower, once you already know what accounts exist to transfer money into. *The Savings Rate Playbook* covers how much to save overall, and, in its own chapter on retirement accounts versus accessible savings, how to split a given savings rate between tax-advantaged and taxable vehicles once both kinds of account already exist and are funded. This book covers the piece that has to come before either of those two questions can be answered in practice: what a brokerage account actually is, how to choose one, what each account type mechanically does, what order to fund things in, what to actually buy, and how to place the trade. A reader with no investment accounts open at all is best served starting here; a reader who already has accounts open and funded and is working through automation or allocation questions is better served by those two companion volumes, returning here for the specific mechanics of fund selection, order types, or rebalancing whenever a given chapter's topic becomes directly relevant.

Readers new to the Wealth Mechanics library are welcome to start with any volume that matches their most immediate question rather than reading in numbered order — each book stands fully on its own, with no assumed prior reading, and cross-references a companion volume only where the territory genuinely overlaps, as flagged explicitly above.

A note on why this particular volume exists at all, since a library covering negotiation, debt, pricing, automation, and savings rate might seem, at first glance, to have already covered the ground of "what to do with your money." Every one of those five prior volumes assumes, somewhere in its opening pages, that an investment account already exists to receive whatever money the book's own framework produces — a negotiated raise, a freed-up debt payment, a calculated savings rate. None of them walk a reader through the specific, mechanical gap between having decided to invest and actually holding an open, funded, invested account. That gap turned out to be large enough, and common enough, among readers of the earlier volumes in this library, to warrant its own dedicated book rather than a short appendix bolted onto an existing one — the vocabulary alone, per Chapter 1, is substantial enough to deserve real, unhurried treatment, not a rushed aside inside a book about something else.

Future volumes in the Wealth Mechanics library will apply the same situation-mechanics-framework-example structure to other closed, calculable domains of everyday money decisions that most people only work through a handful of times in a life, or get wrong the first time for lack of a clear method. Each volume stands on its own and requires no prior volume to use.

## Also in the Series

Every book in Wealth Mechanics stands on its own — read them in any order. If this one was useful, the library continues:

*The Negotiation Playbook*

*The Debt Freedom System*

*The Pricing Playbook*

*The Automatic Wealth System*

*The Savings Rate Playbook*

*The Side Income Playbook*

*The Real Estate Entry Playbook*

*The Tax Reduction Playbook*

*The Equity Compensation Playbook*

www.ingramcontent.com/pod-product-compliance
Lightning Source LLC
LaVergne TN
LVHW010719061126
851857LV00014B/1257
* 9 7 8 1 8 0 4 2 8 1 4 7 5 *